Integrating Hadoop

William McKnight and Jake Dolezal

Technics Publications

Published by:

2 Lindsley Road
Basking Ridge, NJ 07920 USA

https://www.technicspub.com

Cover design by John Fiorentino
Edited by Lauren McCafferty

First Printing 2016

Copyright © 2016 by William McKnight

ISBN, print ed.	9781634621526
ISBN, Kindle ed.	9781634621533
ISBN, ePub ed.	9781634621540

Library of Congress Control Number: 2016950004

Table of Contents

1 Hadoop in Support of an Information Strategy

For decades I've watched the ebb and flow of data and technology keep up with each other. Technology advancements seem to breed data. Then, as more data becomes available, businesses clamor to capture that data and harness it as meaningful information for their enterprise. The hunger for information gives rise to new technologies. It's a never-ending dance.

The advent of social media in the last decade has made available information that formerly didn't exist digitally. The opening of this digital data floodgate has created an opportunity for unparalleled advancements in technology.

For example, affordable sensors that ensure the nonstop flow of digital data are available to supply chains. Internet speeds have increased and coverage has broadened to keep the data flowing. Our ability to use the data—at advanced levels we call this "data science"—has increased tremendously. This is the most exciting time in the digital age!

In 2013 the earth generated about 4 zettabytes (ZB) of digital data. IDC forecasts that we will generate 40 ZB by 2020[1]. Although not all of that data will be used, increasingly more of it will. And it's not just stored once. Data with value is branched off into numerous databases across multiple companies. The amount of data globally generated in the last few years exceeds the sum of all data generated previously.

We're on track to hit 50 billion connected devices! Processors are embedded in things everywhere! Most physical objects are on their way to being online. Internet Protocol 6 will allow for 78 octillion (billion billon billion) simultaneous connections. In a few years, the internet will relatively swell from the size of a baseball to the size of the sun.

Machines are primarily responsible for this explosion of big data. Machine data contains critical insights. It allows us to perform unprecedented triangulation of physical objects, including people! Unlike traditional structured data—for example, data stored in a traditional relational database for batch reporting—machine data is non-standard, highly diverse, dynamic, and high-volume.

The challenge is bringing the data together. We can build a comprehensive picture of activity when we correlate and visualize the related events across these disparate sources.

---

[1] "The Digital Universe in 2020: Big Data, Bigger Digital Shadows, and Biggest Growth in the Far East", December 2012, By John Gantz and David Reinsel.

Companies that can capture and harness this data can benefit accordingly. Industries that are growing fastest are those that are adopting new technologies and using data to understand themselves and their industry.

We can't afford not to store and process more data if we want to be more successful than our peers. Companies know that if they can accurately anticipate a consumer's next move, they have a tremendous advantage in the market.

Business has clear upward trends of spending on big data. It's projected to be the top item of spend in many industries. But, big data is more than Hadoop. For example, graph is a fast-growing database category, and streaming data is becoming more common for real-time data analysis. Both of these involve big data and were barely mentioned ten years ago.

Most companies have to admit that no matter what business they are in, they are in the business of information; everything else they do simply allows them to keep a status quo. Successful businesses can accomplish nothing without an intense focus on the many and growing technical bases that can be used to store, view, and manage data.

The vendor market has kept up with the increasing demand for data. As systems like Hadoop continue to annually double their price-performance, bandwidth, and storage capabilities, amazing business opportunities become obtainable.

"Let no data escape" should become the guidepost for organizations in their approach to data. Every element of data generated has value, either today or in the future. Once it is used for operational purposes, it will be interesting to analytics.

If businesses truly want to embrace the *let no data escape* mantra, they must embrace the following technologies:

- **Hadoop/Spark Ecosystem** – This ecosystem will evolve, but the foundation (scale-out file systems without overhead) and the trend toward stronger non-functionals will not change.
- **Master Data Management (MDM)** – Despite the prevalent resistance to sharing data, efficiently collecting or generating data to share in small and large ways is essential to the bottom line. The generation capabilities of MDM are increasingly being required.
- **Internet of Things** – Though not a technology, a consideration of using the internet as the processing backbone of new applications is increasingly compelling.
- **Cloud** – It's hard to imagine just "cloud" as being a category. At least by listing it here, though, we can view it for what it truly is: a major disruptive force to IT as we know it.
- **NoSQL** – Perhaps this moniker will morph again, away from "not only SQL" to something that doesn't imply its origination as the antithesis of a programming language. Anyway, online digital strategies simply need to process too much information for any other operational approach.

Introducing Hadoop

Hadoop is a technology that was created in 2006 to meet the needs of the Silicon Valley data elite. These companies had data needs that far surpassed any budget for any database management system (DBMS) out there. The scale was another order of magnitude beyond that of the existing DBMS. Companies weren't certain how quickly they should be scaling up, given the variability of data. It's not like Google wanted to be bound by calculations like "by this time next year we'll have 3 petabytes, so let's build to that." They had no idea what was to come.

Hadoop was originally developed by Doug Cutting, who named it after his son's toy elephant. Today, Yahoo is the biggest contributor to the Hadoop open source project. Eventually, the code for Hadoop (written in Java) was placed into open source, where it remains today. However, several companies like Hortonworks and Cloudera have developed versions of Hadoop that falls under closed source. While most enterprises prefer to work with these value-added companies and will pay a premium for them, you can go to http://hadoop.apache.org and download Hadoop without cost.

Hadoop is Not...

... a good choice for processing transactions or other forms of random access. It is best for large scans. Neither is it a good choice for processing lots of small files or intensive calculations with little data.

We have become accustomed to real-time interactivity with data, but use cases for Hadoop must fall into batch processing. Hadoop also does not support indexing or an SQL interface—not yet, anyway. Another reason to avoid it for transactions is that it's not strictly ACID (Atomicity, Consistency, Isolation, Durability)-compliant.

Hadoop is quickly being adopted by diverse businesses from the largest Web-data companies to the Fortune 1000 down to mid-size and smaller companies.

Hadoop will replace little of what organizations now have (and plan to, or could have in the future) in their data warehouses. Sometimes the rationale for thinking about Hadoop is a belief that the multiple terabytes in the data warehouse constitutes "big data" and Hadoop is for big data analytics.

Types of Data Fit for Hadoop

- **Sensor Data**–pulsing sensor readers providing low-granularity activity
- **Clickstream Data**–detailed website visitor clicks and movements
- **Social Data**–internet-accumulated data entry
- **Server Logs**–diagnose processes in detail by analyzing logs
- **Smart Grid Data**–optimize production and prevent grid failure
- **Electronic Medical Records**–support clinical trials and optimize
- **Video and Pictures**–look for patterns in these high-storage and dense objects
- **Unstructured Text**–look for patterns in accumulated text
- **Geolocation Data**–analyze anything by its specific location
- **High-Volume Data**–any that out-scales DBMS value
- **"Cold" Enterprise Data** - with no immediate or known utility.

Sure, the big data of Hadoop is plentiful, but it is not in the data warehouse, nor should it be. It will ultimately be more data by volume than what is currently in the data warehouse– maybe petabytes. This big data is the data we've either willfully chosen to ignore to date or are just beginning to generate.

Hadoop has historically referred to a couple of open-source products: *Hadoop Distributed File System* (HDFS), a derivative of the Google File System, and *MapReduce*. However, the Hadoop family of products continues to extend into an ever-growing product set.

HDFS and MapReduce were co-designed, developed, and deployed to work together. *Spark* can also sit on HDFS.

By leveraging the in-memory capabilities of Spark on HDFS, users can integrate datasets at much faster rates. Spark uses fast Remote Procedure Calls for efficient task dispatching and scheduling. It also leverages a thread pool for execution of tasks, rather than a pool of Java Virtual Machine processes. This enables Spark to schedule and execute tasks at rates measured in milliseconds, whereas MapReduce scheduling takes seconds and sometimes minutes in busy clusters.

Hadoop scales well and relatively cheaply, so users do not have to accurately predict their data size at the outset. Summaries of the analytics are valuable for interaction with the data warehouse.

HDFS is based on a paper Google published about their Google File System. It runs on a large cluster of commodity-class nodes (computers). Whenever a node is placed in the IP range as specified by a *NameNode*—one of the necessary Java virtual machines—it becomes game for data storage in the file system; henceforth, it will report a heartbeat to the NameNode. Upon adding the node, HDFS may rebalance the nodes by redistributing data to that node.

Sharding is a technique for spreading the data set to nodes across data centers across the world, if required.

A *rack* is a collection of nodes, usually dozens, that are physically stored in close proximity and are connected to a network switch. A *Hadoop cluster* is a collection of racks. This could comprise up to thousands of machines.

There is one NameNode in the cluster (and a backup NameNode). This NameNode should receive priority in terms of hardware specification, especially memory. Its metadata about the file system should be kept totally in memory. NameNode failures, while not catastrophic (since there is the backup NameNode), do require manual intervention today.

Hadoop data is not considered sequenced and is in 64 MB (standard), 128 MB, or 256 MB block sizes (although records can span blocks). It is replicated a number of times (three by default) to ensure redundancy (instead of RAID or mirroring). Each block is stored as a separate file in the local file system (e.g. NTFS). Hadoop programmers have no control over how HDFS works and where it chooses to place the files. The nodes that contain data, which are well over 99%, are called *datanodes*. Datanodes are slaves to the NameNode.

The NameNode decides where the replicas are placed. The key factors in this decision are load balancing, fast access, and fault tolerance. Assuming three is the number of replicas, the first copy is written to the node creating the file. The second is written to a separate node within the same rack; this minimizes cross-network traffic. The third copy is written to a node in a different rack to support the possibility of switch failure. Nodes are fully functional computers, so they handle these writes to their local disks.

Unlike DBMS scale-up architectures, Hadoop clusters with commodity-class nodes will experience more failure; the replication, though, makes up for this downfall. Hadoop replicates data across different computers, so that if one goes down, the data is processed on one of the replicated computers. Since there is usually 3x replication, there exist more than enough copies in the cluster to accommodate failover. HDFS will actually not repair nodes right away. It does it in a "batch" fashion instead.

Hadoop Distributions

There are several variations of the Hadoop footprint, with more undoubtedly to come. Prominently, there is open source Apache/Yahoo, for which support is also available through independent companies Hortonworks and Cloudera. EMC, IBM with BigInsights, and the Oracle Big Data Appliance also come with training and support.

Distributions are guaranteed to have components that work together between HDFS, MapReduce, Spark and all of the supporting tools. They are tested and packaged. Given the many components, this is not trivial added value.

Hadoop data integration is complex and is the focus of this book. In the next chapter, we'll get ready for integration, and then we'll discuss the model of ELT (extract, load, transform) for Hadoop data; this will lay the foundation for loading data into Hadoop, which we'll start in Chapter 4.

2 Preparing for Integration

Assembling the Integration Team

Given that staffing is always your largest Hadoop investment, it's important to assemble a team that efficiently brings together all the expertise you need. The core of this team should be your current relational database experts, with leadership coming from IT, data warehouse, and/or BI teams.

Effective Hadoop teams extend outward from this core. By that we mean that teams must not only possess knowledge of Hadoop technologies, but a broad business perspective (cross-enterprise, in many cases) as well. Your team also needs technical and strategic people who fundamentally understand why processing data on Hadoop is birthing a new generation of apps, game-changing business models, and innovative ways to better serve customers.

Roles and Responsibilities

Team roles are similar to those in the RDBMS world, but each has extended requirements. While organizations conceive of roles and combine skill sets differently to suit their specific needs, the descriptions below cover the basic competencies and how they need to stretch for Hadoop success.

Hadoop Administrators

You can prototype Hadoop projects on a couple of machines, but when you're ready for production workloads, you need people who know how to manage jobs across complex clusters of processors—which may be running on-premises, in clouds, and/or in hybrid architectures. You're also likely to need specialists in administering Hadoop components, such as Hive, Impala, and Spark, since it's difficult to find individuals with a high level of competence across all of them.

Traditional DBAs could be good candidates for Hadoop administrators, provided they can make the necessary shift in mindset and are willing to undergo considerable technical training. The learning curve can be steep; although we're starting to see more automated tools, many Hadoop admin processes remain largely manual and thus require strong programming skills.

You can ease the learning curve by utilizing customized Hadoop distributions that incorporate proprietary enhancements. Other options include analytic platforms that combine Hadoop with a massively parallel processing database and tools—generally available as software-only systems, appliances, or cloud services. There are also complete "Hadoop-as a service" solutions: cloud-based packages that handle all installation and administrative tasks for you.

Data Integration Developers

As in traditional data warehouse environments, the overarching need is for people who know how to prepare data for analytics and analytics-infused applications. These are the folks who perform ETL (extract, transform, load) or ELT (extract, load, transform—where the processing-intensive last step takes place in the database).

The difference in the Hadoop environment is that developers are performing transformations and integrations across enormous volumes and varieties of data from an ever-expanding range of sources. Until recently, this required people with strong Java MapReduce skills. Today, with data integration solutions sitting atop Hadoop, people with modest technical skills can perform transformations without writing any code at all.

These visual tools not only expand the pool of potential candidates, but also improve the productivity of all developers, enabling their role to become more strategic and business-oriented. Indeed, one of the most valuable developer skills is the ability to understand the implications of new data types as they become available, and to figure out how to combine them with each other and with existing data to create business advantages.

Data Architects and Data Stewards

Oversight of data quality and governance is especially important in Hadoop environments, where data—flowing to and from myriad end points—is stored without schemas, and there are no limits to potential uses and users. Like Hadoop administration, data stewardship functions may require some programming of manual processes. Increasingly, however, Hadoop data integration solutions incorporate visual tools and consoles for viewing the performance of transformations and monitoring data integration flows.

In addition to administering a data governance framework, this role may also encompass other responsibilities aimed at minimizing operational and reputational risk. Data ethics, for instance, is a growing concern, as big data integration technologies enable organizations to dig much deeper for insights about individual consumers, as well as to derive more attributes, come to more conclusions, and make more predictions from data. Someone on your Hadoop data integration team needs to act as point-person for collaborating with business managers or cross-enterprise committees to define and implement a data ethics policy.

On the other hand, a data architect/steward can also be the point-person for cross-enterprise efforts to maximize upside opportunity from data integration. They can promote practices, for example, that enable reuse of data integration work and champion end-user self-service for data exploration and data-driven business apps.

Data/Application Engineers

These are software engineers developing big data applications that require Hadoop's massively parallel processing. In addition to being adept with Java (and/or other 4th-generation programming languages like Python, Perl, or C++), they must be familiar with the rapidly expanding number of open-source and proprietary tools for Hadoop.

Just as importantly, developers must be able to wrap their heads around the implications of the expanding IoT (Internet of Things) and a whole new class of SaaS apps blooming in vendor clouds. These apps—many of which consume data streaming in from IoT devices, chips, and sensors—are using big data in ways unimagined before Hadoop became mainstream. Many are also generating big data. Your team needs developers who can connect the dots between the myriad new technical possibilities and the business visions, asking questions that start with "What if we could...?" These should be your most strategic thinkers.

Data Scientists

Scientists with the statistical and applied mathematical expertise to analyze data for insights (i.e. to extract signal from noise) are more critical than ever in Hadoop environments. Most Hadoop projects, of course, involve processing a lot of big data to find a relatively minute amount of signal. Because Hadoop can rapidly crunch through enormous amounts of data, it's economically feasible to extract these insights. In addition, scientists may discover patterns that aren't evident in smaller data sets.

These team members investigate the value of various big data sources; in Hadoop environments, this involves mastering a wide range of tools and analytic techniques. Creating queries and guiding machine-learning algorithms, they discover data patterns and relationships that could potentially be useful for BI, or for building predictive or descriptive analytic models. They determine which data looks interesting enough to justify further analysis and build logical views (e.g. Hive tables) on top of the data to facilitate queries by themselves and other users.

Data Analysts

As in the traditional data warehouse environment, data analysts run queries to respond to inquiries or produce reports. Thanks to today's SQL-on-Hadoop solutions, most of their skills are transferable; with the processing performance of Hadoop, they'll enjoy a nice bump up in productivity.

What's different with Hadoop is that the role of data analyst leans more toward internal consulting. You need these data experts to point business analysts and other business users to the right sources, and guide less-technical staff in accessing, integrating, and analyzing data for specific business aims. Data analysts can also help by creating data visualizations that can be accessed from libraries and reused in different contexts (BI tools, mobile apps, web pages, etc.).

Business Analysts

In Hadoop environments, business analysts still fulfill the critical functions of looking for ways to improve business processes, posing questions that can lead to discovering strategies for competitive advantage, and helping to specify requirements for new products and services. They're empowered in all of these responsibilities by an increasing range of role-based, self-service graphical tools that greatly expand their abilities to access, integrate, and analyze big data. In fact, data integration solutions on Hadoop include hundreds of prebuilt connectors to big data sources.

In addition, these tools enable the role of the business analyst to encompass data preparation, including contributing to data profiling, cleansing, and validation processes. Analysts may also be able to help specify and maintain data quality rules under the oversight of the data steward.

Citizen Developers

Hadoop is ushering in a new era of ubiquitous analytics, where nearly every job in the enterprise involves working with data in some respect—ideally via self-service tools or using familiar apps. Forward-looking organizations understand the competitive potential of infusing everyday tasks with evidence, insights and predictions. They're doing everything they can to put big data analytics in the hands of enterprise citizens. As you set up or build out your own Hadoop environment, keep end-users—and the tremendous leverage they can exert as big data consumers—clearly in your sights.

Overview of Workloads for Hadoop in the Organization

Hadoop usage has changed since the advent of technology to make batch-processing big data affordable and scalable. Today, with a lively community of open-source contributors and vendors innovating a plethora of tools that natively support Hadoop components, usage is expanding along multiple vectors.

Here are today's most common workloads as well as the directions in which they're evolving.

Data Preparation

Traditionally, data preparation has consumed an estimated 80% of analytic development efforts. One of the most common reasons for using Hadoop is to drive this analytic overhead down.

Data can be prepared through a traditional ETL process: extracting data from sources, transforming (cleansing, normalizing, integrating) it to meet requirements of the data warehouse or downstream repositories and apps, and loading it into those destinations. As in the relational database world, many organizations prefer ELT processes, where higher performance is achieved by performing transformations after loading (see the next chapter for more about tradeoffs and trends). Instead of burdening the data warehouse with this processing, however, transformations will be performed in Hadoop. This gives you high-performance, fault-tolerant, elastic processing—without detracting from query speeds.

Hadoop environments demand massive processing power, as transformations often involve integrating different types of data from a multitude of sources. Your analyses might encompass data from ERP and CRM systems, in-memory analytic environments, and internal and external apps via APIs. You might want to blend and distill data from customer master files with clickstream data stored in clouds and social media data from your own NoSQL databases or accessed from third-party aggregation services. You might want to examine vast quantities of historical transactional data along with data streaming in real time from consumer transactions or machines, sensors, and chips. (See the next section for more about sources.)

Hadoop can handle all of this structured, unstructured, semi-structured, and multi-structured data because it allows schema-less storage and processing. When bringing data into Hadoop, there's no need to declare a data model or make associations with target applications. Instead, loose-binding is used to apply or discover a data schema after transformation, when the data is written to the target production application or specialized downstream analytic repository.

This separation of data integration processes from the run-time engine makes it possible to:

- Share and reuse transforms across data integration projects
- View data in different ways and expose new data elements by applying different schema
- Enhance data sets by adding new dimensions as new information becomes available or additional questions emerge.

These Hadoop advantages all work to reduce analytic preparation overhead. Used in conjunction with data governance best practices, they can also improve data quality, helping to increase enterprise confidence in analytic results.

Active Archive

Given Hadoop's capacity to store immense amounts of data, one of its early uses was for archiving. With Hadoop, users could afford to keep not only a couple of years of transformed data, but a dozen years of data in both its transformed and original states.

Today it's more economical to archive such rarely used data in cloud services from Amazon, Google, and other vendors. Still, it may make sense to store middle-ground data—infrequently needed but still useful for analytics—in Hadoop. It's a low-cost way to store a lot of data when you want easy access, but you don't mind slower querying speeds compared to relational databases.

Moreover, the tradeoff for slower queries is increased agility: Your "long tail" of data can be easily remixed with new data to yield new analytic insights or fuel new types of user apps.

Analytics

It's estimated that most enterprises analyze only about 12% of their data.[2] Hadoop has the potential to substantially expand that pie slice. It's becoming cost-effective to analyze more and more internal data, increasingly in combination with external sources of big data as well.

Some of this expansion will be fueled by more people analyzing more big data. While data scientists and analytics developers will still perform complex explorations and model building, SQL-on-Hadoop tools will enable data analysts, business analysts, and other business users to work with big data.

A growing use case for Hadoop is data mining, with machine learning available to help different kinds of miners. Scientists can take advantage of Hadoop's processing speeds to run sophisticated algorithms, accelerating data discovery along a path. Experts can guide the way and assist in identifying the most predictive data relationships for modeling. Data analysts and business users can rely on machine learning to suggest potential data schema, expose potentially interesting data relationships, and guide them in constructing basic analytic scorecards.

Fueled by the Internet of Things, demand for streaming, real-time analytics is exploding. Soon many consumer and business products will be sending data throughout their lifecycles to vendors and manufacturers. Using Hadoop, the recipients can analyze this data on the fly, including in the context of other internal (in-memory and stored) and external data. Streaming

[2] Forrsights Strategy Spotlight BI and Big Data, Q4 2012, Forrester Research © 2012 Forrester Research, Inc.

analytics are also important for real-time customer behavioral profiling and prediction, and for anomaly detection in the realm of cyber security.

Data Quality/Governance

Only three in ten organizations trust the data in their analyses, according to a study by Ventana Research[3]. One of the main reasons cited was the inability of environments to readily adapt to changes in data types and sources. Another was lack of holistic data quality standards and governance. Clearly Hadoop's flexibility can help organizations address the first problem, but flexibility without adequate oversight can also amplify the second problem.

Fortunately, there are an increasing number of ways to improve data quality and governance. The Apache Falcon component, for instance, provides policy-based workflows as well as metadata services for tracking data lineage and usage. In addition, dedicated data integration solutions on Hadoop now incorporate fine-grained monitoring of ETL-ELT processes, drag-and-drop data quality tools, and automated processes for data matching and de-duplication, validation, and testing. Some include management consoles for monitoring data flows from development through production, with automated rule-based alerts and reporting of data quality issues.

---

[3] Ventana Research, "Delivering Trusted Information for Big Data and Data Warehousing: A Foundation for More Effective Decision-Making," July 2012.

Data Virtualization

The ability to separate data integration processes from run-time engines on Hadoop supports data virtualization techniques. You can generate semantic views of data structures that allow users to transform, move, and analyze data without having to know the technical details about where the source data is actually located and how it's formatted. This technique is similar to data federation, except that on Hadoop, it's unnecessary to impose a data model.

Virtualization can simplify both front-end and back-end processes. At the front end, by abstracting multiple data sources through a single data access layer, users can create data services for specific business purposes. Users focus on the big data views and analyses that are relevant and useful to them. At the back end, virtualization improves performance by reducing disk I/O and eliminating unnecessary replication.

Another advantage of virtualization is that it can help knock down the silos. By creating virtual data structures over legacy applications and databases, you can open up a set of data while still controlling who can access it and how it can be used.

These advantages come together impressively in prototyping. Developers working on data warehouse changes or analytic apps can map data services across any number of sources and construct a data movement process without actually moving data. When it's time to convert prototype to production, they can push a button to perform integration on the fly and load the data set into the data warehouse, target app, or downstream analytic environment.

Data Lakes and Beyond

The data lake is an emerging concept that builds on Hadoop data abstraction and separation of processes. The key innovation is that the data doesn't move at all. It's never loaded into a data warehouse or downstream analytic repositories. It stays in Hadoop, and the various run-time engines process and analyze it from there. This concept has been described as bringing the computation to the data instead of bringing the data to the computation.

The key advantage of this approach lies in its potentially much lower processing and analysis costs. By eliminating data replication and movement, you also reduce opportunity for errors, thereby potentially improving data quality and governance.

Most organizations experimenting with this new approach are creating data lakes that coexist with data warehouses. Some people, however, believe that data lakes will someday replace traditional data warehouses and other repositories. They see the lake as the basis for a software-defined data center that provides a unified view ("data fabric") of all data across the enterprise, and centralized control over access and use. Some even expect Hadoop to evolve into a data operating system, robust and full-featured enough even to encompass MDM (master data management) functions.

Identifying Data Sources for Hadoop

There are innumerable sources of big data, and more springing up all the time. Here are some you may want to explore:

NoSQL Databases

With the advent of big data, a wide variety of non-relational database approaches have become popular for their abilities to scale across clusters of processors and to store unstructured or semi-structured data types. Examples include:

- Columnar databases such as Cassandra and HBase
- Graph databases such as Neo4j and InfiniteGraph
- Document stores such as Clusterpoint and Couchbase
- Key-value caches such as GigaSpaces, Terracotta, and Velocity
- Key-value stores such as Hyperdex, Aerospike, and Oracle NoSQL.

Legacy/Relational Databases

Operating system data, including from enterprise resource planning (ERP) and customer relationship management (CRM) systems, can be accessed and integrated from mainframe legacy databases and relational databases via Hadoop. So can data warehouses, which were traditionally built on relational technology. Examples of proprietary relational databases include:

- Oracle
- IBM's DB2
- Microsoft's SQL Server.

Open source examples include:

- MySQL
- PostgreSQL
- SQLite.

Clickstreams

As website visitors click through pages, their browsers generate a series of page requests, which are transmitted back to servers in streams. With each click, a range of data—typically including date, time, user ID, browser, operating system, country, city, requested URL, and hostname—is recorded. This data is available from web analytics vendors, such as Google, Amazon, and Adobe. However, you can also use analytics tools, such as Snowplow Analytics, to capture clickstream data yourself.

Sensors

An increasingly ubiquitous source of machine-generated data, sensors are being put into everything from wearable fitness devices to home smoke alarms, automobile parts to factory robots. In this growing IoT, sensors, chips, and devices will constantly stream data to servers while also communicating with each other to enable increasingly sophisticated functions and deeper, more contextual data analysis.

APIs

Application programming interfaces (APIs) are the predominant way of accessing data from cloud-based data services, databases, and apps. These are sets of routines, protocols, and tools that enable software programs to request services from other programs. Examples include APIs for Google Maps, Facebook Graph, and Versium, a vendor that uses social media APIs to correlate consumers' email addresses with their social networking activity for behavioral analysis, then makes the resulting analytic insights available to customers via its own API.

Data Profiling

How do you select the right data sources? The first consideration is, of course, source relevance and fit to your purpose. Apart from that, sources vary widely in quality and granularity of the data—both of which have a major role in determining the extent of data transformation your project will require. These characteristics are revealed by data profiling (see next section). In general, the profile of a good source will show:

- a typographical error rate below your specified threshold
- a low percentage of incomplete and incorrect data fields
- a high degree of conformance to standard patterns (e.g. zip code format) and, where applicable, to industry-standard taxonomies
- an adequate use of metadata to make data structure and characteristics easier to understand.

Analyzing and Profiling Source Systems and Data

Given the expanding range of data types from a plethora of Hadoop-compatible sources, data profiling is more important than ever. Profiling is essential at different stages of analytic development, including:

At project inception, to...

- explore candidate data sources to understand how they're structured (or not) and the level of detail they encompass

- assess data quality and the nature and degree of anomalies that will need to be addressed
- determine if the data fits your analytic and applications needs.

Prior to ETL/ELT, to...

- identify the data to be extracted
- select filters to apply
- design transformations.

Prior to analytic modeling, to...

- determine whether adequate data is available for modeling
- assess what will be required to build a model from the data.

Data integration solutions for Hadoop include data profiling tools. Capabilities should include:

- **statistical profiling** to generate record counts and data quality metrics (blank fields, null values, duplicates, unique values, most/least frequent values, etc.)
- **textual analysis** for developing profiles of text fields (min/max length, average length, etc.)
- **numeric analysis** of the values in numeric fields (ranges, quartile distributions, etc.)
- **frequency tables** showing how often different values occur
- **pattern analysis** to assess data for conformance with standardized patterns like email address syntax, postal address syntax, credit card number formats, or your own custom formatting rules.

Now that data is ready for integration, in the next chapter we'll weigh the decision between ETL and ELT; then we'll continue on to loading and managing data in Hadoop.

3 ETL versus ELT

ETL (extract, transform, load) and ELT (extract, load, transform) are both acronyms for three-step processes that move data from one place (and purpose) to another. Generally, data from multiple source systems is being moved to, and consolidated in, an enterprise data warehouse (EDW) or other target database(s), where it becomes available for further use.

The important difference between ETL and ELT is in the transformation step. In this step, data is cleansed, put into formats/structures required by the EDW or downstream datamarts and apps, and normalized and integrated so that it can be compared, merged, and analyzed with data from other sources. When using ETL, these tasks are performed through automated tools or hand-coded scripts prior to loading. With ELT, the bulk of transformation is completed after loading, inside the HDFS, data warehouse, or other target database. Pre-transformations can take place in the source database as well.

Continued Need for More Speed

Changes in how and when data is transformed have occurred gradually over the past couple of decades, and continue today. They are spurred by the ever-expanding volume and variety of data that businesses need to consolidate, and all the new ways in which they want to view, analyze, and use it.

In the mid-to-late 1990s, when ETL processes first showed signs of having trouble handling growing transformation workloads within allocated time windows, ELT emerged as an alternative. It made sense to take advantage of increasingly powerful RDBMS (relational database management system) architectures. Some incorporated MPP (massively parallel processing) for the heavy lifting. Database tables from source systems were loaded directly into a staging area in the EDW, where SQL was used to perform the transformations.

But as data volumes continue to grow, all that batch transformational processing—which an RDBMS wasn't originally designed to do—slows down the processing of queries for BI and user apps for which it was designed and optimized. In addition, the SQL-based transformation logic requires a lot of maintenance to keep up with changing data and user needs.

Many organizations, whether utilizing ETL or ELT, are solving the speed and transformation problems by offloading some or all of the "T" step to a Hadoop-compatible file system. Using MapReduce to distribute transformation workloads across hundreds or thousands of servers on industry-standard hardware, users gain elastic performance and scalability for data integration while improving query speeds on the freed-up RDBMS.

Hadoop also increases reliability and throughput rates for transformations by improving fault tolerance. If your servers go down in the middle of a transformation, the work is redistributed and doesn't have to be rerun. If you discover a mistake in ETL/ELT logic after the fact, you can rerun past transformations without slowing down current jobs, by temporarily adding more servers to process the extra work.

Preference with Hadoop

The preferred approach with Hadoop is ELT, since it fully leverages the technology's strengths. Consider the role of ELT with Hadoop in two important data management and integration trends:

Bring All Data Together

Today your business wants to capture and combine not only structured data from diverse sources, but unstructured data that's even more varied. Competitive advantage might emerge from layering behavioral data from customer transactions with attitudinal data from comments or blog posts.

In this case, your "E" step will increasingly need to encompass text, images, audio, and video, as well as streaming data from sensors, network events, and other machine-generated sources. Since Hadoop is the most efficient way to persist and process such a mix of data, it makes sense to load unprocessed or largely unprocessed data, and then perform the transformations in Hadoop.

Keep All Data Now (Decide How to Use It Later)

With Hadoop's ability to store and process massive amounts of data rapidly and inexpensively, it's no longer necessary to make up-front decisions about which data is most valuable and how it must be used. ETL processes, essential in the past for selecting data that seemed important and assigning it to a data schema before loading, can be limiting in this new era of virtually unlimited capacity. If one of your business groups suddenly has a need for data that was not included in the original preconception, the schema must be amended and ETL logic revised.

There is still the extraction from source, but instead of instant transformation, the raw data can be loaded into the repository—in this case, HDFS. The load process does not require a schema and the transformations can be applied later, upon usage or transfer to another platform like HBase.

ELT processes are better suited to business environments where continuous and disruptive change makes it impossible to predict which data will be important next week, tomorrow, or later today. In these environments, it's best to store everything you can get your hands on, then use loose binding techniques to apply or discover schema ("on read") when data is needed for specific application development or analytic projects. This approach makes it much easier for your IT organization to respond to ad-hoc integration requests. It also provides the necessary foundation for increasing the amount of self-serve integration and analysis your "citizen developers" can process independently.

Is ETL Dead?

The short answer is "no." ETL will continue to play a role in many enterprise data environments. For one thing, the need to move an enormous set of structured data into an EDW or another target database very quickly will still exist; using an existing ETL process could be the most efficient way to achieve this.

From a broader perspective, ETL tools are evolving. Some can now orchestrate transformations inside of Hadoop, an RDBMS, or an in-memory system. With its ability to push transformational logic to the best place for each job, at whatever point in the data flow and lifecycle makes sense, ETL is becoming more of a "ETLT" hybrid. It's an approach that's likely to gain adherence as the Hadoop-enabled notion of "move the computation to the data" rather than "move the data to the computation" becomes more widely accepted and practiced.

4 Loading Data into Hadoop

Advantages of Data Integration Tools

As with any task or trade, it is important to have good tools for the job. Robust, powerful, efficient tools can make all the difference in the speed and quality of any work. Big data integration is no exception.

One of the chief benefits of big data open platforms, especially Apache Hadoop, is that they are relatively inexpensive. However, low prices have their own hidden costs: complexity, steep learning curves, development and support talent, longer time-to-value, etc. Therefore, an enterprise looking to step into or maximize an investment in big data and Hadoop should leverage good tools to lessen the "costs" or trade-offs of a big data implementation.

The first advantage offered by big data integration tools is simplification of coding across the big data landscape. Hadoop, MapReduce, Spark, real-time streaming, and NoSQL are all powerful animals, but they are *different* animals. Each requires different knowledge and native coding abilities. A big data integration application or environment must have a solid graphical interface with widgets and wizards that generate native code in each of the different environments. A robust abstraction layer with visual, easy-to-customize components enables an enterprise to move data to and from different technologies, to begin harnessing their individual strengths. Talend Big Data, for example, offers this capability. Hand coding, or acquiring the talent to code across all the different big data platforms, can be costly in terms of time and budget. This cost can be mitigated by choosing a robust data integration tool.

The second advantage of a data integration platform is that it provides the thread for weaving big data into the entire information fabric of the organization—regardless of the enterprise's architecture. Big data implementations need not be experimental or siloed efforts, separate from the core information management architecture. Big data can be brought into existing decision-making engines and processes, with the help of a data integration tool with a healthy set of connectors and components to hook big data into existing BI and analytic efforts.

However, this isn't just a one-way street. Big data integration toolsets for enterprises can be used with the same rigor and solid data management practices utilized everywhere else within the organization. Tools allow organizations to manage big data while they move it—loading, transforming, enriching, and cleansing, both inside and outside Hadoop. A solid integration tool should also provide shared repository and metadata capabilities, as well as the capacity to perform data profiling and matching. This makes it possible to distribute, manage, and govern big data just like any other data within the enterprise.

Methods of Data Loading

While a robust data integration engine offers all these advantages and capabilities, we need to walk before we run. A great place to start is loading data into Hadoop. There are a variety of methods for loading into Hadoop—each one offering its own fit-for-purpose.

Batch

The original method for loading data into Hadoop (the one for which it was designed) is batch loading. Batch is the meat and potatoes of data integration with Hadoop—a staple fit for many of its early and continuing use cases. Batch loading was designed specifically to help in situations where a very large set of data is acquired, or data sets are frequently received, and these large volumes of data must be dealt with.

Conventional approaches to batch loading data onto Hadoop involve HBase. Another member of the Apache Software Foundation, HBase is a non-relational database that sits on top of HDFS. Batch loading of data requires at least some form of a database management system, since HDFS only manages files in their native state (typical of a file system). HBase was designed and remains best suited for sparse data: data laid out in rows and columns having NULL values for most columns (i.e. in the 90-99.9 percent range). Storing this type of data in a traditional relational database is an inefficient use of resources and results in poor performance.

Row	Col1	Col2	Col3	Col4	Col5
1	NULL	NULL	val	NULL	NULL
2	NULL	val	NULL	NULL	NULL
3	NULL	NULL	NULL	val	NULL
4	val	NULL	NULL	NULL	val
5	NULL	NULL	val	val	NULL

An example of sparse data, for which HBase was designed.

During a batch load, tables in HBase serve as the inputs for MapReduce jobs run in Hadoop, and are usually accessed through an API. The basic steps for a batch load of data into Hadoop are as follows:

1. Load the data file into HDFS
2. Parse the data with a MapReduce job
3. Send the data to HBase through an API.

However, some data integration developers elect to utilize Hive[4] as an intermediary at Step 2 (above). This is because Hive runs SQL-like queries, making it easier for developers with SQL experience to easily achieve the same end results using queries and routines with which they are very familiar (e.g. CREATE TABLE).

Real Time

The alternative to loading data in batch is to load data in real time. Many analytical use cases require the analysis of the most current data *as it happens*—not a post-analysis of data that has

---

[4] Hive is Hadoop's version of a data warehouse designed for SQL-like querying, summarization, and analysis of data.

accumulated over the past few days, as is the usual case for batch loading and conventional data warehouse ETL. Thus, the value of data is realized by capturing it in its real-time stream or constant flow, as opposed to backing the data truck up and dumping it in one load at a time, then sifting through the heap.

To perform real-time data loading in Hadoop, a streaming engine must run on top of Hadoop. Earlier engines included Apache Storm and Kafka—both developed in 2011 by LinkedIn and Twitter, respectively. However, the innovative advances of Apache Spark and Spark Streaming, boasting higher performance and ease of use, have quickly made Spark a frontrunner for the streaming engine of choice for big data integration.

Streaming engines and real-time streaming data integration will be discussed in greater detail in Chapter 8: Streaming Data.

Sqoop

The information management architecture for big data will undoubtedly contain relational databases (RDBMS) as sources (and targets) for data coming into (and going out of) Hadoop. Enterprise resource planning (ERP), customer relationship management (CRM), point-of-sale (POS) systems, and similar systems may all serve as sources of information for a Hadoop cluster.

The tool for this job is another Apache project called Sqoop. Apache Sqoop was designed to transfer bulk data between Apache Hadoop and structured data stores—specifically RDBMS and legacy mainframes. In addition to loading data, Sqoop can also be used to extract data from Hadoop and export it into a number of RDBMSs or appliances, including Teradata,

Netezza, Oracle, MySQL, and Postgres. Sqoop has three basic functions:

- Import (reading the RDBMS data row-by-row)
- Generate code (MapReduce code that can be reused)
- Export (parse the HDFS data into records and insert them into the target).

Sqoop is robust and powerful. However, it does have a drawback. Sqoop by itself is activated by command-line interface only. For a graphical user interface, you must use Apache Hue (a Hadoop web browser-based console and management tool) or a data integration tool that leverages Sqoop.

Nifi

Apache Nifi is an Apache addition that holds tremendous promise for sourcing IoT data. IoT devices with data to be captured create pressure on the data target. In our models, this target is Hadoop.

If your source is a relational database and you are sourcing in batch, Sqoop is still the way to go. Its parallelism will provide the best performance. Otherwise, there are a ton of connectors built for Nifi (i.e., HDFS, Hive, RDBMS, Kafka etc.) to take advantage of, with Sqoop-like functionality just the start.

One area Nifi excels at is user friendliness, thanks to a highly-configurable advanced user interface that provides drag-and-drop data movement similar to relational ETL.

With Nifi, unwanted data is filtered out at source, security is applied to the entire flow and, most importantly, changes are captured from real-time queues along with rich metadata, eliminating data lag as well as design challenges.

Nifi allows the setting of prioritization for how data is retrieved from queues. The default is oldest first, but there are times when data should be pulled newest first, largest first, or some other custom scheme. Data is removed from Nifi's content repository as it ages off the content repository or as space is needed.

Change Data Capture

Any modern architecture involving data integration should include mechanisms for change data capture. There are several methods for achieving change data capture and incremental loads into Hadoop.

First, the chosen method will depend on the source system and how it identifies changed or new records. Is it a "last-modified-date," a control flag, an audit or history table, or some other method? Also, what is the target for the data—an HDFS file or a Hive table? Answering these questions will help determine which incremental load and change data capture strategy you ultimately choose.

As an example, let us assume we have a source RDBMS and a target Hive table (this is akin to a conventional data warehousing environment). In this case, you would use a four-step strategy:

Step 1. Load incremental data into a separate Hive table using Sqoop.

Once Sqoop completes an initial load of the source into what we will call a Hive "base table," subsequent incremental loads can be loaded into a separate "incremental table." The Sqoop code for such a load would look something like this (assuming a Teradata source and using a "last-modified-date" control attribute):

```
sqoop import
    --connect jdbc:teradata://[host
    name]/Database=[Database Name]
    --connection-manager
    org.apache.sqoop.teradata.TeradataConnManager
    --username [Username] --password [Password]
    --table [Source Table]
    --target-dir /user/hive/incremental_table -m 1
    --check-column modified_date
    --incremental lastmodified
    --last-value [Last import date]
```

Sqoop also has a "query" parameter, so you can write an actual SQL statement to select the changed records, if you prefer:

```
sqoop import
    --connect jdbc:teradata://[host
    name]/Database=[Database Name]
    --connection-manager
    org.apache.sqoop.teradata.TeradataConnManager
    --username [Username] --password [Password]
    --table [Source Table]
    --target-dir /user/hive/incremental_table -m 1
    --query 'select * from SOURCE_TBL where
    modified_date > [Last import date]'
```

Step 2. Create a view that combines and reconciles the base and incremental tables.

The two Hive tables—base and incremental—need to be combined together and reconciled. This can be achieved with a Hive SQL Union and Group By, based on key fields and the last-modified-date attribute, to only show the updated records in the union of the base and incremental records.

Step 3. Create a new base table from the view.

The third step is simply to create a new base table from the reconciled view from the previous step. In Hive, you can use a SQL statement such as CREATE TABLE [new base table] AS SELECT * FROM [view], and then replace the old base table.

Step 4. Clean up.

In many instances, this step simply involves dropping or deleting the incremental table. In HDFS, you could easily drop the table through a file system command, such as:

```
hadoop fs -rm -r /user/hive/incremental_table/*
```

Push versus Pull

As with any architectural decision, another data integration question is, "Do you want to push or pull?" Hadoop allows for both types of methods; you'll have to determine the best method based upon your use case, architecture, and the types of sources you have.

In terms of the data you want to integrate into your Hadoop cluster, you must ask, "Do we want to be driven by events being pushed to us, or does it make more sense to poll and scour for events and pull them in?" If, operationally or analytically, your business is event-driven, your Hadoop architecture should be set up for a push data integration method. If you need to poll and fetch needed data or data of interest from a generator, you should implement a pull methodology in your big data integration environment.

Path to Production

Once a big data integration solution is built and becomes a working prototype, it still needs to be put into production. Planning tools take a role in determining the "path to production," which refers to the steps necessary to vet the solution, make it more resilient, and bring it up to standards, procedures, scheduling, supportability, and other aspects of good data integration management.

Workflow and Scheduling

Scheduling batch loads of bulk data into a Hadoop cluster can be achieved with Oozie. Another Apache Foundation project, Oozie is server-based and manages workflows that schedule and coordinate tasks and jobs on a Hadoop system.

Oozie workflows are written as XML files. The workflow consists of a start point and an end point, with actions and decisions in between. A basic workflow XML skeleton looks something like this:

```
<workflow-app xmlns='uri:oozie:workflow:0.1'
    name='example'>
    <start to='step1' />
        <action name='step1'>
                Actions would go here.
                <ok to='step2' />
                <error to='fail' />
        </action>
        <action name='step2'>
                Actions would go here.
                <error to='fail' />
        </action>
    <end name='end' />
</workflow-app>
```

Once your workflow is created, another XML file, known as a coordinator, needs to be created to actually schedule the workflow application steps to run on a certain frequency—using the Unix *cron* syntax. A coordinator XML to execute an Oozie workflow every night at 11:30PM looks something like this:

```
<coordinator-app name="example" frequency="30 23 *
 * *"
 start="2016-01-01T05:00Z" end="2016-12-
 31T06:00Z" timezone="UTC"
 xmlns="uri:oozie:coordinator:0.5">
 <action>
    <workflow>
       <app-
 path>hdfs://localhost:8020/tmp/workflows</app-
 path>
    </workflow>
 </action>
</coordinator-app>
```

Unless you enjoy writing and validating your own XML, another option is to use a robust data integration tool, such as Talend Studio, to generate this code for you. An example with screen shots for scheduling a data integration job using Oozie and Talend is provided in the next section.

Support and Troubleshooting

Another consideration prior to bringing your big data integration solution into production is the support maturity of your IT organization, and how they can help troubleshoot problems within this realm. Unless your IT team is made up of Hadoop "natives" (i.e. fluent in the language) and experts, it may be necessary to extend your support circle out to a consulting team, or even vendor partners for your particular Hadoop distribution or data integration tools. Having someone to call on—whether internal or external—when things do not go well, or to overcome technical hurdles, is a reassuring safety net.

How-To with Talend Big Data

The following section demonstrates how to use Talend Open Studio for Big Data to load data into Hadoop as an example of tool usage. Before beginning to create your own jobs, you have to configure the connection to a Hadoop cluster in your Talend repository. See the *Talend Open Studio for Big Data User Guide* for more details.

One-time Batch

To load data into Hadoop with Talend, begin by creating a job and defining its basic properties.

In this example, we will load a delimited text file into Hadoop—the simplest of all cases. We'll first add a component that will represent the file to be imported. By searching for, and selecting the tFileInputDelimited connector in the palette, we can drag it onto the workspace and start building our job.

Note that you can also insert components right onto the canvas by selecting the workspace and typing the name of the component you want (once you get familiar with your favorite Talend components).

Then, drag a tLogRow component onto the canvas to monitor the data being processed. The third component is a tHDFSOutput component to transfer the data to HDFS. To run this job, we also need a tHDFSConnection component. Everything is connected together, and the final job looks like this:

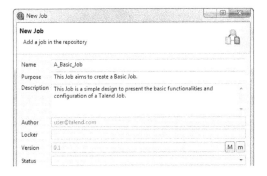

Scheduled Batch (Oozie)

Talend Open Studio for Big Data provides an Oozie scheduler, a feature that enables you to schedule executions of jobs, run them on an HDFS server, and monitor the execution status of the jobs. Like before, you must first define the HDFS connection details in the Oozie scheduler settings, and specify a path where your job will be deployed.

After entering your environment's settings, click "OK."

To schedule a job, simply click the "Schedule" button on the Oozie Scheduler pane.

Enter the Frequency with an integer, and select a time unit (e.g. hour) to define how often the job should run.

Next, Click the "..." button next to Start Time and select the date, hour, minute, and second values you desire. Click "OK," and set the job execution end time in the same way.

The job will now automatically run with these parameters.

Relational Dump (Sqoop)

Talend also makes dumping data from relational databases into Hadoop fairly straightforward, thanks to Sqoop. In this example, a tLibraryLoad component is connected to a tSqoopImport component.

The tLibraryLoad component is used to load a Java archive (jar) file that can be used by the job to read data from a MySQL database.

The tSqoopImport component actually connects to the source database by specifying the connection credentials and the table to go after—in this case, "contacts."

5 Managing Big Data

Big Data ELT

From an architecture standpoint, data integration is evolving in a major way, quickly becoming the solution to today's big data challenges.

The first evolution we've seen is the migration from proprietary, commercial, all-in-one products to open source platforms powered by tools like Spark and Storm.

The second evolution involves one of the classic hallmarks of ETL products: the ability to connect to a wide variety of systems and platforms. Today's big data integration solutions are gracefully traversing the tightrope between the SQL/NoSQL and RDBMS/non-relational chasm.

The third evolution is within the ETL development environment. Conventional ETL tools had highly-refined, graphical user interfaces, but big data saw a return to good old-fashioned coding, as drag-and-drop, palette-based development environments were not available. Plus, big data ETL development involved coding for an API or through a high-level Domain Specific Language, like Hive or Pig. A return to coding challenged the necessity of traditional graphical interfaces for ETL development, but recent innovations brought back the capability, bridging the coding gap for many organizations.

Transformations

In the previous chapter we saw how the extract and load process of ETL/ELT play out. Now, let's look at transformation.

When creating big data integration, it is important to remember that Hadoop cannot natively perform ad-hoc joins and data aggregations. Therefore, multiple transformations are required to pre-compute data in preparation for a new data set, or to create the view expected by end-users and their preferred query patterns. For example, in a NoSQL platform like MongoDB or Cassandra, the same aggregation will appear across several rows and collections by different dimensions and levels of granularity.

Those familiar with conventional data warehouses are also familiar with the star schema, a structure that analyzes a business process based upon a core set of measures viewable at different levels of granularity. However, in big data "warehouses," dimensional data must be "denormalized" or flattened in order to connect facts with their dimensional attributes. The consequence is more transformations and an increased payload for big data ETL jobs to materialize the alternate views of data.

Not only are we now processing massive data volumes, but we must process more often, potentially creating a vast amount of processing overhead and technical debt if not managed properly. Therefore, the challenge for the data architect is scale. Conventional tools were designed for an environment where single node processing was the only reality; they could not scale to the rapidly expanding data volumes of the big data era.

When designing transformations in the context of Hadoop, you must first understand the nature of your workloads: do they require complex methods germane to relational databases? If your job requirements include joining three or more tables, creating temporary tables, or doing multi-passes of the data, you'll need to plan accordingly. In the case of ELT (or extract, load, transform), your conventional ETL tool will usually push all this relational processing down to RDBMS. Hadoop is an unlikely candidate to support this type of workload without help.

On the other hand, if the job demands only basic relational capabilities, it can be easily managed using an HBase row store or a Hive table. If no relational capabilities are needed, then MapReduce should be sufficient.

Data integration requirements that call for simple aggregations and calculated values (but at massive scale against millions of records) are perfect candidates for the Hadoop environment. Remember that Hadoop was created by companies who lived and breathed the Internet, where simple but massive numbers of aggregated clicks, page views, and ecommerce transactions were required. For transformation workloads resembling this type of requirement, going "all-in" with Hadoop is your best bet.

"Upserts" within Hadoop

A powerful and popular big data feature that must be considered is the "upsert." An upsert in conventional RDBMS allows a data integrator to safely insert a new row or update an existing row on the basis of the row already existing. The use cases for upserts are so common—their use is essentially expected in any data integration project. With big data, the upsert functional need presents several challenges, but also several opportunities with their own respective trade-offs.

First, Hadoop itself is an immutable file system and has no update command. So how can an upsert be performed without an update capability? When ingesting data, Hadoop was designed to append new sets of data at the event or sub-transactional level. The event or sub-transaction data itself does not change; it just flows in large quantities over time. However, to produce any analytical value, this data must be combined with reference or dimensional data—data that will change over time.

Handling merges, upserts, and slowly (and sometimes not so slowly) changing dimensions in Hadoop is challenging. In conventional ETL and RDBMS environments, it is easy; those experienced with these functions will have to rethink their strategy. The good news is there are multiple options and methods to tackle an upsert in Hadoop.

Rip and replace

The first method makes use of the tool (and conventional SQL logic) to perform the upsert off Hadoop, and periodically copy the refreshed data into Hadoop, via Sqoop, replacing the previous version of the file on HDFS. The upside is that all the hard work (e.g. complex update rules, Type 2 slowly changing dimensions, surrogate keys) is done by the tool. Thus, the Hadoop file is ripped and replaced with the newly "upserted" information.

This method is easy to carry out and the most straightforward for Hadoop novices. However, the downside is that this method is not scalable. Once reference tables become large, load performance will degrade. Another disadvantage comes with the prospect of maintaining separate environments (Hadoop for batch loads and RDBMS for maintaining dimensions) and orchestrating the workflows between them. With shorter and shorter windows for extraction requirements in more global businesses, the processing load times and orchestration will reach its limits of scalability very quickly.

Use HBase

HBase provides native support for updates. Tools like Talend provide HBase components for lookup, insert, and updates, making it a strong candidate method for performing upserts. HBase can also be used in real-time streaming applications with low latency, while the rip and replace method above cannot. The choice now seems simple, right?

Well, not really. The problem with HBase arises on the back end, when analysis is performed. HBase is, unfortunately, poorly suited for analysis. Querying HBase is optimal when only a single row or a range of subsequent rows are selected. If a full scan of the table is needed, HBase performance breaks down. In fact, even a simple GROUP BY query of file-based data in HDFS can outperform the same query in HBase. As such, if you need to perform upserts into dimensional tables but have very few backend analysis requirements of the dimension, the HBase method may be your best bet.

An example of an HBase upsert in Talend Studio using the tMap, tHBaseInput, and tHBaseOutput components is shown below.

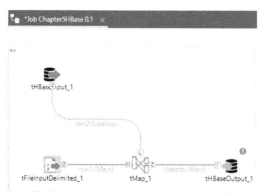

Change data capture

The third upsert strategy is to use the change data capture method presented in the previous chapter. Incremental changes to be upserted are loaded into a separate Hive table using Sqoop, and then a view that combines the new data and the old via a UNION and GROUP BY is created, to allow the updated records to cover up existing ones. Finally, a new dimension table is created from the view, and unneeded files are cleaned up. For more details on this method, refer to Chapter 4: Loading Data into Hadoop.

The drawback to this method is the read/write overhead that is created every time an upsert routine is run; the entire dimensional table must be read and processed, even if only one record is upserted. Real-time updates will not work using this method, either.

Choosing the right upsert strategy is a matter of several factors, including: the size of your dimensions, the windows you have for extraction and batch processing, the amount and speed of volatility in your dimensions, and the complexity of your upsert rules.

Importance of Data Quality in Hadoop

As big data becomes more and more important, so do solid big data management practices. With all the integration, transformation, process orchestration, error recovery, and data redundancy pieces of the big data puzzle, data quality becomes more critical to organizations. Not all Hadoop use cases are for analytics, but most have that component; this makes data quality an important consideration when Hadoop's output is used for analysis and decision making.

The first question that must be asked is, "Can data quality practice scale to the same levels as Hadoop?" Hadoop obviously pushes the limits of analytic data storage to the sky—not only in terms of data volume and variety, but also in structure. Maintaining quality of a conventional data warehouse, by virtue, has always meant limiting the volume, variety, and structure of data allowed. With the promise and capacity of Hadoop, data quality was initially overlooked by management.

The next question logically follows: "Does the same data quality practice *need* to scale to Hadoop?" Statistically, "bad data" may not be as bad as it once was. The effects of a statistical outlier or anomaly are reduced by virtue of the massive amounts of data that drown it out. In conventional data analysis and data warehousing practices, "bad data" was something to be detected, cleansed, reconciled, and purged, as not to taint the data store. People are naturally resistant to the idea of poor-quality data being present in their analytics, even though it is always a reality to face. Rigorous data hygiene measures and practices are put into place, including record-by-record manual correction of data in order to purify sources and analytical stores.

However, the volume and variety of Hadoop makes these traditional data quality practices impractical. Remediating row by row in a Hadoop store would take an army of data custodians; this would hardly be worthwhile, given the low business value density of big data. Generally, it's useful to think of big data as a *big* picture view rather than a *perfect* picture view. However, in certain cases, the accuracy of the data going into or coming out of Hadoop may be critical to the success of a project. In that case, more vigilance is required.

The solution, in any case, is to turn to a data integration tool with data quality components and capabilities. Used in combination with data quality and stewardship portals, the data quality components included in the ETL tool help detect and mitigate data quality issues *en masse*.

Stewardship of Big Data

The discipline of data stewardship, which includes managing data quality and information throughout its lifecycle, is a mature practice—although not all organizations apply them with an equal fervor. If big data is an extension of the information ecosystem, should the same data stewardship practices be applied? The worst application of data stewardship concerning big data is to simply ignore it and do nothing. In this section, we will discuss possible techniques to fold big data into your existing data governance program.

Folding into Existing Data Governance Process

Despite the overwhelming scale of big data, applying data stewardship is not impossible. Hadoop includes a variety of data hygiene approaches to enforce data quality standards and rules. The nature of the data, its usage, and its application will dictate the amount of cleansing needed (which sometimes is none at all). You may elect to use any of the following techniques, or a combination:

Accept and limit

The first technique is to accept the reality of bad data, but ensure its frequency remains within a tolerable limit. One principle we alluded to in the previous section is that the net collection of a large array of sources with enough good data will drown out the effects of bad data. In statistics, the larger the sample size, the less misleading an outlier or anomaly will be.

This is a fairly passive approach, but also is the *de facto* choice of early Hadoop adopters. To enforce data stewardship, trending and threshold analytics must be performed on certain measures with the data set. This analysis should monitor an expected range of good data or occurrences of known "bad data," and track whether or not the norm is drifting.

Correct and improve data

The second method utilizes more data science. The idea is to leverage data scientists to not only analyze data, but correct and improve its quality as well. This is not to say that expensive, elite data scientists must be recruited. However, scientists can apply the same methods they use to explore and experiment with data to track quality.

Pre-process data

The third strategy is to apply some data rules at a pre-ingestion state, before a new data set is batch written to Hadoop. For instance, say you have a data standard that all dates appear in YYYY-MM-DD format. A regular expression (Regex) script could be written to find errant dates and replace them with the correct format. This would ensure that at least some elements going into your Hadoop store are consistent, saving analysts time later.

Cleanse at consumptions

The fourth technique is to cleanse data at consumption, rather than at ingestion. The collection of big data often involves the collection of meaningless data that will likely never be used. Big data analysis often entails the art and science of finding the signal within this noise. Once the signal (meaningful data) is found, focus data cleansing activities on this smaller data set.

Analyze bad data

The final technique is not to ignore, discard, or cleanse bad data, but to actually analyze it. Bad data can be insightful. "Why is the bad data bad?" is a valid and important business question. Bad data can be used to spot something amiss, to indicate that "normal" conditions are shifting, or as a leading indicator that something is about to happen. Data from a sensor on a mechanical machine, shifts in temperatures, or even customer sentiment analysis could fall into this category. This type of analysis has the capacity find something critical just in time. In this case, bad data may actually be good.

Metadata

In the Hadoop world, native metadata storage is part of Hive and is called HCatalog. HCatalog is a level of abstraction that gives users a relational view of data in HDFS, regardless of the format in which the data is stored. HCatalog is a technical solution, but is not necessarily enough to apply your organization's metadata standards to your Hadoop data store.

To apply metadata standards to your big data, define the entities and attributes of those entities within your data store, including:

- Business terms and definitions
- "Primary keys" or identifier attributes
- Data quality rules (to be applied via the technique chosen in the section above)
- Change data capture rules (to identify whether a record has changed).

Don't forget to account for the changes and evolution of the "schema" of incoming big data over time. If a third party source changes the layout of their file, you will have to manage those metadata changes.

6 Unloading/Distributing Data from Hadoop

Hadoop Extracts

In a robust data architecture, Hadoop can serve as a source or hub for data distribution. Some professionals in the space may refer to this as a "data lake." The concept of a data lake has received much attention in recent years; basically, a data lake is a massive repository for storing the majority of an organization's data to be used for analytics.

Architecturally and technically, Hadoop can serve this purpose. Whether or not your Hadoop instance is considered a data lake is immaterial. Regardless of the particular arrangement of Hadoop and how it sits in your overall information management architecture, you will undoubtedly encounter cases where data must be extracted from Hadoop and put on another platform.

Hadoop data can be off-loaded or extracted and placed virtually anywhere that can handle the volume. The following section discusses the techniques most useful in moving the data off Hadoop.

Relational, Operational, and Legacy

For most modern relational database management systems, Sqoop Export will be the most direct and straightforward method to pull data from Hadoop and store it in RDBMS. Basically, any database management system that supports Java Database Connectivity (JDBC) or has a JDBC driver can take advantage of this technique. This includes everything from Microsoft SQL Server, Oracle, MySQL, Vertica, Netezza, Redshift, and DB2 iSeries, down to Access and comma-separated values (CSV) files. There are also third-party ODBC drivers if your DBMS does not support JDBC.

The simplest use of the Sqoop Export technique can be performed in one line of code. For example, the following Sqoop command at the terminal prompt can move Hadoop data into MySQL (provided the appropriate permissions are granted within MySQL):

```
sqoop export --connect
    jdbc:mysql://localhost/database --table
    customer -m 1 --export-dir
    /user/hduser/customer
```

In Talend Studio for Big Data, the tSqoopExport component is used in conjunction with a tLibraryLoad, which allows a user to specify a database connector JAR file.

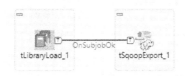

For operational systems, the requirements and techniques for loading data from Hadoop may be the same. However, appropriate development and testing methods are recommended to ensure that the Sqoop jobs running in production are producing the desired results, particularly on key operational systems that carry your business' critical workloads.

Legacy systems (such as mainframes) that do not have JDBC (or ODBC) drivers will require an intermediary step. Typically, these legacy systems will have a native import function. You will have to design a Hadoop export that transforms the data into whatever format the legacy import function expects. Refer to your legacy system documentation.

NoSQL

Although not typically used for integration, data can be moved from Hadoop onto a NoSQL platform, such as Cassandra or MongoDB. Sqoop can be used, with custom modifications—and some NoSQL vendors have done this. However, the recommended method is to use a data integration tool that has the *in* and *out* connectors for the NoSQL platform you are using. This method ensures the highest data integrity and greatest ease in coding.

Typical use cases for a Hadoop-NoSQL tandem would be to use Hadoop to offload or archive old records from your NoSQL system. In this case, you may desire to have a "put back" mechanism, or a way to push the data to another NoSQL instance designed for analytical use cases.

Data Warehouse

The enterprise data warehouse (EDW) has always been a way to distribute summarized transactional data for analytical purposes. The capabilities of Hadoop make it tempting to replace an enterprise data warehouse with an HBase or Hive warehouse. Some organizations are making that choice, for reasons such as controlling cost and enabling larger scale or processing power. However, there are several trade-offs to consider:

First, finding people with talent and skill in Hadoop is challenging. There is not an overabundance of professionals with vast experience writing MapReduce in Pig, Java, or other programming languages that require specialized knowledge. The technical know-how required even to write ad-hoc queries and perform basic analytics make it a barrier to business user communities used to writing SQL against a data warehouse. An IT shop that seriously knows its stuff must be heavily involved, helping business users meet their needs. This is not a recipe easily followed.

Second, the enterprise data warehouse handles certain types of analytics really well, and it organizes the data in a sensible way for the average user. Whether it is aggregating sales numbers by region, channel, or product line, slicing customer survey data by dimensions, or producing profit-and-loss or risk analysis, the data warehouse is still king. The pre-defined schemas and data marts provide consistency and familiarity that business users enjoy. Ripping that ease-of-use and replacing it with something more challenging is not likely to engender a ton of early adopters.

Third, most data warehouses are already configured and have a multitude of adapters to connect to systems across the enterprise. Your enterprise resource planning (ERP), point-of-sale (POS), customer relationship management (CRM), and other systems crucial to your business likely already feed your data warehouse on a daily basis. That feeding mechanism was not built overnight.

Complex ETL jobs that run in tight overnight windows have been built and refined. Not to mention all the reports that have been built and are delivered to your business users; they expect and depend on these to complete their jobs. It would be expensive and possibly very painful to rewrite all those integration jobs and reports to point at the new Hadoop data warehouse. Even if that were your intent, you'd quickly run into the first problem again: finding enough strong arms to carry that load forward quickly.

Instead, many companies are electing (and many consultants and analysts are recommending) to use Hadoop to augment—not supplant—their existing enterprise data warehouses. By erecting the Hadoop warehouse architecturally alongside the existing warehouse, organizations can enjoy new capabilities and insights by combining the power and strengths of both platforms. Here are some suggestions for successfully enabling a dual conventional and Hadoop EDW architecture:

1. Continue to use the conventional data warehouse to transform and store summarized and aggregated structured data from your transactional and back office systems. This includes atomic attributes and

dimensional slicers of transactional data: quantities, dollar amounts, dates, identifiers (customers, products, regions, etc.), flags, and other highly-structured transaction attributes.

2. Use Hadoop to store raw, unstructured data that does not fit neatly into the star schema fact and dimensional tables that are part and parcel to your conventional data warehouse. This includes: auto-transcribed phone logs, customer feedback statements and sentiments, global positioning coordinates, photographs, tweets, emails, and so on. This type of data can be stored in a very cost-effective way in Hadoop.

3. Correlate the data from the two systems together and link the data by the identifiers for your customers, products, locations, transactions and other master data.

This one-two punch will greatly increase your analytic capabilities and will introduce loads of rich insights into your business' conventional aggregated dimensional analysis and reporting. You'll get the best of both worlds.

Regardless of the architectural decisions you make, do not build Hadoop within a silo. Aim for a combination of Hadoop and legacy analytic platforms; this will enrich the value of the latter by adding the new data volume and variety capabilities of the former. Many data warehouse and appliance vendors have added Hadoop to their offerings.

However, if you are considering Hadoop as a cost-cutting measure to replace an expensive or bloated legacy data warehouse platform, a transitional strategy will be needed. The progression will involve building up the Hadoop capabilities and cutting over from the old EDW in a strategic and politically-sustainable way, with an eye constantly on the organizational change management ball.

MDM Hub/360-degree View

In the world of big data, one of the greatest challenges is identity resolution. You may collect vast amounts of feedback, sentiment, geo-location, event-driven, and other types of big data, but unless it can be tied back to an individual customer, visitor, product, transaction, or other entity, it can be difficult to correlate the data to achieve targeted, specific, full-circle insights.

Master data management (MDM) is the management of critical data elements about entities like customers and products. MDM is also in the business of identity resolution, which uses algorithms to help businesses understand who is who and what is what.

Many companies use MDM for risk management and fraud detection. Others use it to improve customer service and communication by expunging duplicate, outdated, or incorrect data. Leveraging big data for master data management offers some exciting capabilities.

New algorithms within data integration and MDM tools are matching entities through indirect association. For example, a matching algorithm might identify a person through a common phone number or by associating households through marriage. Big data can greatly augment these efforts. Many vendors have coupled their big data integration and match-merge master data management transformations into the same application.

Beyond identity management, the combination of MDM and big data is a means to cultivate data from sources like the web and social media, creating a much more complete customer "360-degree view." In the past, companies would purchase potential customer data from Dun & Bradstreet or Nielsen, and think they had a 360-degree view, while in fact, those companies provided only a narrow view. By augmenting the customer 360-degree record with data from outlets like Facebook, Twitter, and LinkedIn, the customer view is greatly enhanced.

Using the MDM components within your data integration tool can bring unstructured data alongside traditional structured data. Using this data, you may be able to infer extremely insightful data about a customer—everything from their hobbies and beliefs to their favorite sports team. All this data is valuable fodder for salespeople who want to more closely engage with their potential customers.

Hadoop and SOA

Service-oriented architecture (SOA) has been around for decades, but the idea of an enterprise hub or bus for big data is new. Big data vendors have attempted to position themselves as enterprise data hubs, placing Hadoop at the center. For organizations that already have a SOA in place, Hadoop integration can be tricky.

Service-oriented messaging middleware is not unchartered territory for the Hadoop ecosystem. Apache Mule is a project that implements an enterprise integration pattern, and the Apache ActiveMQ project adds to Mule with additional capabilities. Additionally, Apache Camel uses an API on top of a similar enterprise integration pattern, to configure message routing and rules. For example, Talend offers an Apache Camel tool and graphical user interface.

Additional vendors and projects are hoping to leverage YARN as an enterprise service bus (ESB), but to date, nothing sustainable is available on the market. The most direct integration route for Hadoop in SOA depends on whether your ESB supports connections with Hadoop and has native connectors to perform messaging and data movement.

7 Apache Spark Cluster Computing with Hadoop

Advantages of Real-Time Computing

Real-time computing in information management represents data-driven decision making with a real-life time constraint; either the "freshness" of the data has an expiration date soon after acquisition, or a decision needs to be reached *now* and not a few days from now. Sometimes real-time responses from data are needed in a matter of hours, minutes, or even seconds. In these cases, performance is key; if data cannot be compiled and analyzed to guarantee a response within the specified timeframe, it cannot offer real-time computing and decision making capacity.

In terms of conventional data integration practices, improving performance involves batch processing data within a given window of extraction, processing, and loading to ensure that data collection is "cut off" by a certain time (usually at night), and then made available to the business again by the time the next business day begins. For data warehouses and business questions where yesterday's data is "good enough" for today's decisions and analysis, utilizing only data integration from the batch-processing perspective is also good enough.

However, more and more business questions and analytical use cases are requiring quick answers. Many of those questions also require the use of big data. With increasingly larger volumes of data and narrower decision-making and integration windows, performance is not just key, it is make-or-break critical.

Even with the voluminous potential capacity that cluster computing provides in terms of disk storage, there is another shared resource we can leverage: memory. With memory providing read and write access rates to the order of thousands of times faster than disk, leveraging memory for data integration is critical to meet the high performance demands of real-time computing and analytical environments.

Spark

In 2009, the AMPLab at the University of California, Berkeley, started an open source cluster computing framework capable of in-memory processing. They initially called the project "Shark," but later renamed it "Spark." The project was donated to the Apache Software Foundation, where it remains one of the most active open source projects on the entire open source landscape.

To say that people are excited about Spark would be an understatement. It has generated much industry buzz.

According to Black Duck Open Hub metrics, Spark has crossed thresholds of 1,000 individual contributors and 1 million lines of code and comments. By contrast, Apache Hive had a decrease of 66% in contribution activity over 2015.

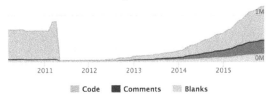

Apache Spark contributions since its open source inception in 2010. Chart ©2015 Black Duck Software, Inc.

The power of Apache Spark is performance. Spark uses multi-stage in-memory processing. What does "multi-stage" mean? Compare it to the two-stage disk-based processing used by MapReduce. In the Map stage of MapReduce, data is read from stable, disk-based storage (i.e. HDFS). The data is then processed, sorted, shuffled, selected, and sent to the Reduce stage. Finally, the data returns to a state of stable, disk-based storage. This cycle repeats itself as the output of the first MapReduce on-disk becomes the input for the next one.

The developers of Spark basically decided to bypass the read-write to disk between processing jobs, by holding the output of the first processing task in cached memory and passing it directly to the next task. According to the AMPLab developers, Spark can perform certain jobs up to 100 times faster than MapReduce.

Consider the power of this processing for data integration. Spark allows applications to load data into a cluster's memory and reuse it repeatedly. For data integration jobs with multiple integration and transformation steps, the data does not need to be written and reread from disk (unless too large to fit in-memory) multiple times; thus, disk I/O is virtually eliminated, except at the front and back ends of the job.

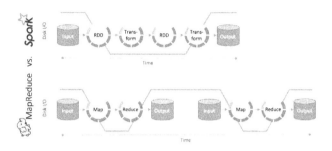

The workflow of MapReduce compared to that of Spark.

Apache Spark comes with cluster-distributed task dispatching, scheduling, and basic I/O functions. At the heart of Spark are the Resilient Distributed Datasets (RDDs), which are logical collections of data partitioned across machines. RDDs can be processed in parallel across a cluster; as such, the more nodes a cluster has, the greater capacity and performance Spark will afford.

For data integration, users and applications create RDDs by loading external datasets via Python, Java, Scala, or R objects. Once an RDD is loaded into memory, the data can be processed via transformations or actions. A transformation results in a new RDD, while an action computes some result and returns it to the application or to external storage. This type of processing activity makes Spark a perfect fit for data integration applications.

The other Spark-enabled capability that boosts the performance of data integration is persistence. By persisting RDDs in cache, the datasets can be used again and again. However, there will be instances when the dataset (or combined datasets) will be too large to fit in-memory, even in a large cluster. For these cases, Spark provides several levels of persistence to allow the user or application to decide how to store and maintain data throughout its lifecycle. The choice of the persistence level has performance and memory tradeoffs.

Spark Persistence Level	RDD Storage State
NONE	RDD is not cached
MEMORY_ONLY	RDD is cached in memory, without replication
MEMORY_ONLY_SER	RDD is cached in memory in a serialized form
MEMORY_AND_DISK	RDD is stored in memory first, spilled over onto disk if too big to fit
DISK_ONLY	RDD is written to disk only
OFF_HEAP	RDD is cached in memory, but outside the Java memory (JVM) heap

Apache Spark RDD Persistence Levels

Clearly, Spark is *not* always doing everything in memory—it just tries to keep as much data and processing in memory as possible. Many data processing engines take the pessimistic view that anything that *can* go wrong *will* go wrong, but Spark is optimistic that everything will go fine. When it does, optimal performance is achieved by skipping all the checkpoints and disk write/rereads.

However, Spark keeps its optimism in check. Spark keeps track of dependencies between its RDDs and can recompute data that falls through the cracks. So take confidence in the output of your Spark jobs. You can always establish post-processing integrity checks, if desired; then again, this incurs another time and performance trade-off.

With its in-memory, processing, and persistence capabilities, utilizing Spark for data integration offers many performance advantages by leveraging the full capacity of a cluster environment. With so much shared memory, why not use it? Certainly you would expect performance gains of in-memory, real-time processing—but just how much?

Spark Benchmarks

Apache Spark has proven itself to be a high-performance tool to leverage Hadoop through data integration. Two benchmarks of Spark highlighted here compare its integration speed to that of comparable Apache Hadoop projects.

In 2014, the AMPLab at the University of California Berkeley executed a big data benchmark[5] that compared query response times for Apache Shark (the predecessor of Spark) in-memory versus several other big data query engines (Redshift, Impala, Hive via YARN, and Tez). In all their use cases with the highest number of row counts (to the magnitude of greater than 80 million rows), Apache Shark in-memory outperformed all the other big data tools. In the case of Shark versus Hive, the query response times were anywhere between 5 and 12 times faster, depending on the query executed and specific use case.

In 2015, MCG Global Services executed a big data benchmark using two leading data integration applications to mimic real-life scenarios in which an organization might integrate data

---

[5] The results of the UC Berkeley AMP Lab benchmark can be viewed at https://amplab.cs.berkeley.edu/benchmark/.

with Hadoop[6]. The benchmark's highest magnitude of data was 12 million rows, from a transactional system integrated with 20GB of log files on a standalone Hadoop instance in the Amazon Web Services Cloud. One product tested was Talend Studio 6, which uses in-memory cache sources and targets to leverage Apache Spark directly. Its performance was compared against that of another industry-leading data integration tools using Hive. At the time of the benchmark, leveraging Spark through Hive with the second application was not supported (and even produced erratic results). The benchmark found that the Talend-Spark integration jobs outperformed the competitor's tool using Hive by 8 times.

Experience has shown that data preparation typically consumes roughly 80% of analytic time and effort. Preparation through traditional ETL process—extracting data from sources, transforming it (cleansing, normalizing, integrating) to meet requirements of the analytic needs or downstream repositories and apps, and loading it into such destinations—can be a time-consuming process. When integrating large data sets of mixed varieties (relational, structured, semi-structured, unstructured, etc.), performing the transformations in Hadoop can spare the data warehouse.

However, with larger data sets, the performance of more primitive Hadoop tools (like HDFS and Hive) degrades and creates integration jobs that can take hours, or even days, to execute. Using Spark on Hadoop can drive this analytic overhead down. This partnership yields high-performance, fault-tolerant, elastic processing with shortened query execution times.

---

[6] https://info.talend.com/hadoopintegrationinformatica.html.

How and Where to Use Spark

Spark has a variety of applications and capabilities within an information ecosystem. Despite its promise and growing popularity, it still has trade-offs and limitations. The key is to identify the right purpose for Spark in terms of appropriate and optimal use cases.

Spark requires a supporting cluster manager and a distributed storage system in which to operate. For cluster management, Spark has a standalone mode (a Spark-only cluster), or it can utilize Hadoop YARN. For distributed storage, Spark can be placed on top of several systems, such as a Hadoop Distributed File System (HDFS) or a service like Amazon S3. The following are examples of common Spark usages.

HDFS

From inception, Spark was designed to read from and write to HDFS. Basically, the deployment depends on whether you are running YARN:

- Not running YARN–You can run Spark in standalone side-by-side with MapReduce (a very simple deployment, especially for those running Hadoop 1.x) or SIMR (Spark in MapReduce) where Spark jobs are launched inside the MapReduce engine.

- Running YARN–You can run Spark on YARN, giving you the advantage of being able to enjoy integration across the entire Hadoop stack, instead of being dependent on MapReduce.

In Talend Studio, the following example shows data from a tCacheIn Spark component being dumped directly into HDFS. The tHDFSConfiguration component must be present in order to configure the job to point at your HDFS cluster.

S3

Spark can also leverage Amazon S3 scalable storage to read from and write to the Cloud. Spark passes the AWS credentials in order to read or write data from S3. This is especially useful if you store source data in S3. When accessing very large datasets, performance trade-offs occur. The following example shows a tCacheOut Spark component reading a delimited text file on S3. In this case a tS3Configuration component is needed to supply your Amazon Web Services S3 bucket, as well as your access key and secret key for authentication.

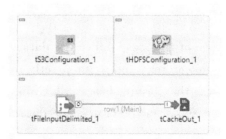

Files

Spark can also read files directly from the local machine (or virtual machine). If your file uses a path on the local file system, the file must also be available at the same path for all the worker nodes. Either copy the file to all workers or use a network-mounted shared file system, so the identical path resolves for all workers.

Databases

Accessing databases is another way you can leverage the power of Spark for data integration. There are a few things to keep in mind that highlight the difference between Spark and relational databases, like MySQL.

Most RDBMS applies "schema on write," and thus must convert the data into its native format to be queried. By applying "schema on read," Spark (as well as Hadoop) can apply a table structure on top of an input file (even compressed text) and see it as a table. Therefore, RDMBS is for storage plus processing, while Spark is for processing only. This is why Spark can pipe data directly to and from external datasets. With Spark able to see data "as a table," it can also query it using Spark SQL—a component on top of Spark that uses a data abstraction layer known as DataFrames.

Taking advantage of these capabilities, a data integration tool like Talend Studio can read and write directly to RDBMS from Spark, as shown in the example below, which filters rows from a Cassandra source and drops them in a Teradata data warehouse appliance.

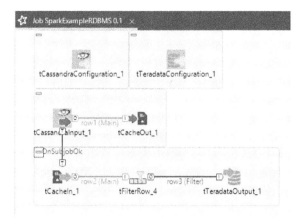

Streaming Analytics

Spark Streaming leverages the rapid scheduling capability of Spark to perform streaming analytics. It ingests data in tiny batches and performs RDD transformations each bit. That way, the same code written for batch analytics can be used in streaming analytics on the same system. This is a powerful feature for those wanting to transition certain workflows from batch to streaming for real-time computing demands and use cases.

8 Streaming Data

Big data is worth talking about, given the analytical value it brings to an enterprise. This is value that is realized and capitalized after the data has been analyzed and made useful for decision-making purposes. While the analysis happens at some point after the data is captured, it's obvious that businesses prefer analytic insight to come sooner rather than later. There is even a metric for this: *"analytic time-to-value."*

There is a special category of big data that has time-sensitive value. If the data is not captured and analyzed in a certain window of time, its value is lost—along with the resulting business decision and action. This category of big data is known by several names: streaming, live feed, real time, event-driven, and so on. Streaming data needs special attention in order to process quickly enough to reap its benefits. For example, a sudden price change, a critical threshold met, a rapidly changing sensor reading, a blip in a log file—all these are red flags that could be of immense value to a decision maker…but only if alerted in time to affect an outcome in the enterprise's favor.

There exists a plethora of big data technologies designed to handle large volumes of time-sensitive streaming data. Each of them was intended to be a managed, real-time, event-driven processing system on top of a highly elastic, scalable infrastructure like Hadoop. They are alike in their objective to process massive amounts of streaming data generated from social media, logging systems, click streams, Internet-of-Things devices, and so forth. However, they also have a few distinct strengths, and weaknesses.

Streaming Data Technology Distinctions

One of the better known streaming data processors is the Apache Kafka project. Kafka was first created by LinkedIn; it was open sourced and graduated from the Apache Incubator in late 2012. Kafka is noteworthy because of its use by big names in the industry. Data-driven technology companies like LinkedIn, Netflix, PayPal, Spotify, and Uber all have previously or are currently using Kafka.

In short, Kafka is a distributed publish-subscribe messaging system that maintains feeds of messages in groups, known as topics. Publishers write data to topics and subscribers read from topics. Kafka is a distributed system; topics are partitioned and replicated across multiple nodes in the cluster.

Within Kafka, messages exist as simple byte-long arrays that can store objects in virtually any format—most often strings or JSON. Kafka makes it possible to attach a key to each message, so that all messages with the same key will arrive together within the same partition, or be delivered to the same subscriber.

Kafka's idiosyncrasy is how it treats each topic partition like a log file where the messages are ordered by a unique offset. To be efficient and scalable, Kafka relies on subscribers to track their location within each log. As such, it spends its processing resources supporting a large number of users and retaining huge amounts of data with little overhead.

Kafka has its imitator: Amazon Kinesis. Kafka and Kinesis share much of the same functionality, but with one distinction. While Kafka is fast and free, it requires a developer to turn it into an enterprise-class solution via installation, management, and configuration. Amazon rolled out Kinesis as a managed, pre-configured, nearly out-of-the-box ready tool with the speed and scale of Kafka, but without the administrative overhead. Another difference lies is nomenclature. Kinesis calls "shards" what Kafka calls "partitions," and Amazon uses the shard in its pricing model. Users pay for Kinesis in terms of shard-hour and payload.

Another similar streaming big data technology is Apache Flume. Flume, like Kafka and Kinesis, is a service for collecting large amounts of streaming data flows—particularly logs. However, Flume is different because it pushes data—also called "data sinks"—to consumers, whereas Kafka waits for consumers to pull data at their own pace. Kafka has an advantage over Flume by providing event replication; if a node goes down, the others will pick up the slack and still make the data available. This is not the case with Flume. If some use case is so mission-critical that data loss is unacceptable, then Kafka is a safer bet.

However, Flume offers the ability to push data to many popular sinks right out of the box, including HDFS, HBase, Cassandra, and some relational databases. Thus, it's much easier to get started with Flume, as opposed to Kafka, wherein users must basically build a subscriber base from scratch. Many commercial Hadoop providers offer Flume in their distributions.

Apache Storm is another project that involves streaming data. It is different in that it serves as the glue between batch processing (which is Hadoop's strong suit) and stream processing (for which Hadoop was not designed natively). Storm is a general event processing system that addresses the gap left by Hadoop. Storm continuously processes a stream of incoming data, while a Hadoop job runs with a fixed amount of data in batches. In Storm, data sources are called "spouts" and each processing node is a "bolt." Bolts perform computations and processes on the data, including pushing output to data stores and other services.

The following diagram represents the basic streaming data architecture and data flows.

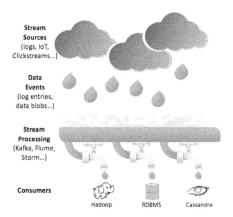

9 Master Data Management and Big Data

We have discussed at length the loading of data into Hadoop, often citing the reasons and purposes for doing so. But, one less obvious value proposition lies in how Hadoop data can interact with the master data of an organization. Increasingly, we see this master data being stored in a master data management hub.

Master data could encompass customers, products, store locations, or anything else that is essential to the business and is shared among multiple systems.

The more heterogeneous the environment becomes—and it should become pretty heterogeneous over time—the more important threading common data elements throughout the environment becomes.

Master Data Management is a discipline essential to obtaining a single, consistent view of an enterprise's core business entities– customers, products, suppliers, employees, and others. MDM solutions enable enterprise-wide master data synchronization. Some subject areas require input from across the enterprise.

MDM also facilitates the origination of master data in a process known as governance (not to be confused with enterprise data governance). Business approval, business process change, and capture of master data at early points in the data lifecycle are critical to achieving true enterprise master data.

One venue of master data management is the data warehouse. Of course, when you view information as a corporate asset, you will see the need to extend it to as many areas as possible to reap its full benefit. Even ERP with its *"everything in one system"* promise should not be the sole venue for master data management. ERP, like many systems, manages just the master data it needs to function, lacking governance and strong, real-time, enterprise-wide distribution capabilities. We've yet to meet an ERP project with an enterprise view. True MDM requires a holistic approach for the enterprise.

When master data is built in a scalable, sharable manner—such as with a master data management approach—it will streamline project development time and reduce the time it takes to get new systems up and running. Reducing scope also reduces project risk.

The ultimate benefit of MDM comes from leveraging the same master data across multiple systems in the enterprise. While this benefit is far greater than that gained by using the total cost of ownership (TCO) "build once" approach, it is more difficult to measure. Regardless, there are definitely efficiencies to be gained by eliminating the contention and correlation of numerous "versions of the truth."

For example, prior to MDM, one client spent 80% of their "campaign development" time poring through competing product lists to determine which one was the true list for the set of products to be promoted. This left little time for the value-added creativity of the campaign. It also elongated development cycles to the point where time-to-market opportunities were routinely missed. Providing a solution for a problem like this is of critical importance.

Master data management is based on a "build once, use often" principle that efficiently leverages corporately-adjudicated, useful data to applications across the enterprise. This means that a little investment goes a long way.

This investment may include simple core attributes, such as a customer's address, but complex attributes as well. An example of complex analytical data is customer lifetime value, which can be calculated and continually maintained in the master data management hub. Complex attributes might call for data to be sent to the hub for computational purposes, but only data to be mastered is stored in the hub. Advanced uses of MDM include transaction data in this way.

Hadoop and Master Data Management

So it seems that we could have quite the investment in master data! What does this have to do with Hadoop? Master data can make the data stored in Hadoop viable in an organization. There is a connection between enterprise MDM and big data.

According to survey results published in November 2012 by The Information Difference Ltd., an MDM consulting and research company in London, 17% of the 209 corporate respondents in North America, Europe, and Asia said they expected big data applications to generate new master data in their organizations. The relationship was much more interesting in the other direction; 59% said they thought big data systems and MDM hubs could be linked together for business uses, including the ability to use master data to automatically detect customer names in sets of big data.

59% claimed the two disciplines are linked, with only 7% seeing no link between MDM and big data. Respondents indicated that the leading way in which the two could interact would be for an MDM hub to provide the master customer data that could help drive web traffic analysis, looking for multi-channel behavior.

67% of survey respondents saw MDM driving big data, rather than the other way around; just 17% saw big data producing new master data. Ultimately, the most popular method was to use MDM data to help drive big data searches.

Integrating with Master Data

Given the possibilities, it is surprising that the actual integration of the two disciplines has barely begun. However, with the value proposition so high, we are focusing on that as a use case category here for you.

One way to achieve the fusion of master data with big data is to bring the master data into the Hadoop cluster through the integration techniques described in this book. With the master data in the cluster, the data could easily be queried together, bringing new life to the usually low value per record of Hadoop data. This would enable real-time transactions with master data, which could be much more than master lists. Extensive analytical attributes could be included in the master data.

Master data together with data typically found in Hadoop can produce:

- More accurate customer risk scores, which allow a bank to better manage its exposure and to offer each customer better products and advice based on customer master data.

- More successful ad displays based on business analysis that incorporates master data reflecting the performance of individual ads and customer demographics.

- Accurate information about the likelihood of a telecommunication customer churn based on how often they use their handsets, how frequently they replace them, and market data about the introduction of new devices by handset manufactures—all found in master data.

- Improved compatibility scores for dating and other matchmaking sites, by combining master data containing information with demographic and web activity (structured and unstructured information) to build a comprehensive picture of its customers.

- The ability to forecast demand and improve the return that a retailer gets on promotional campaigns through integrating master data that has incorporated legacy and new data into its list.

Data Virtualization

Another architectural option is to leave the master data alone in its relational database—referred to as the "hub"—and use data virtualization to join the data as needed.

Data virtualization isn't a new capability. Historically, it was used to circumvent the moving of data into the data warehouse that traditionally would have been physically cohabitating with the other data warehouse data. Unfortunately, it failed to meet expectations. The resulting cross-platform queries, built into the technical architecture as a need, tended to be slow. This brought doubt to the notion of a cross-platform query, which is a far greater need today as organizations have a wider variety of heterogeneous platforms from which to choose.

Fortunately, the technology has caught up and deserves a second look. There are standalone data virtualization tools, some degree of data virtualization built into many business intelligence tools, and even platforms. Some of the built-in data virtualization tends to be limited in focus to support only close technology partners to the technology it is built into.

Data virtualization has the only "bird's-eye view" into the entire (structured/unstructured) data ecosystem:

1) Seamless access to all of the data stores that have been identified with the virtualization tool, including Hadoop and master data management hubs

2) A federated query engine.

Data virtualization is used primarily to provide integrated business intelligence, something formerly associated only with the data warehouse. Data virtualization provides a means to extend the data warehouse concept into data not immediately under the control of the physical data warehouse. Data warehouses in many organizations have reached their limits, in terms of major known data additions to the platform. To provide the functionality organizations need, virtualizing the rest of the data is necessary.

Something virtual does not normally physically exist, but based on the judgment of the tool and the capacity of its cache, the tool may actually physically create the desired structure. Regardless, at some point it has to "join" the data from the heterogeneous sources and make it available. Virtualization refers to querying data that is not guaranteed to reside in a single physical data store, but may as a result of caching. Check to see how intelligent the caching mechanisms of your chosen virtualization platform are. Some will rival the temperature sensitivity capabilities of a robust DBMS.

While some tools provide a user interface useful for those odd queries you may want to run, combining data virtualization with a business intelligence tool (or as part of a business intelligence tool) allows users to continue utilizing the tools they are familiar with for their single-system queries.

MDM is built to govern data and distribute master data. The distribution of MDM data has a significant architectural aspect. MDM data does not have to be physically distributed to a similar structure residing in the target system that wants the data. Depending on the frequency of access and the concurrency requirements on the MDM hub itself, MDM data can stay in the hub and be joined to data sets far and wide in the No-Reference Architecture. Ultimately, MDM will be the highest-value usage for data virtualization.

When the structure you wish to join MDM (relational) data with is not relational, you may create a separate relational store for use with the non-relational data (which would still necessitate data virtualization), or you can utilize the main MDM hub for the data virtualization.

MDM data can bring the value of Hadoop data up immensely. Hadoop has low-granularity, transaction-like data without information—except perhaps a key—about company dimensions (such as customer). Those transactions can be analyzed "on the face" of the transaction, which is of some value; the value of bringing in relevant information not found in the transaction, though, is much more valuable.

For example, you can analyze a person's movement within a store using sensor devices. While this has some value for designing the layout of the store, it is not helpful in marketing campaigns. However, if you know the specifics about a customer such as: "Mary Smith, who lives at 213 Main Street (an upper scale geo), has a lifetime value that puts her in the second decile, has two kids, and prefers Nike clothing," then you can make targeted offers to your customer.

MDM and Hadoop Disconnects

Whether it is virtually or physically cohabitating, the pairing of Hadoop data and master data is not free from complications. MDM brings a dimension of "permanence" to an application, whereas big data projects are sometimes considered more temporal. The juxtaposition of these opposing viewpoints can create confusion in the project development cycle.

10 Top 10 Mistakes Integrating Hadoop Data

1. Integrating Data Without a Business Purpose

It's not enough to just do something; whatever you're doing must truly matter. Integrating data should happen because we want to capture data in a structure suitable for both immediate and long-term uses. Decisions must be made to prevent redundancy of data in the integration process.

For example, it would be foolish from a cost and maintenance standpoint to store data "just in case." Things would soon get out of hand with that reasoning, even if an army were deployed to maintain it. Integrating data into Hadoop usually happens because the data volume to be stored, and the pace at which that data can be generated, are high. Also, this does not mean the data will not need to be integrated and accessed elsewhere at some point.

Whenever you integrate data, there should be a business purpose for having the data accessible. Sometimes, however, the purpose is not readily apparent. In those cases, you must judge whether the timing is right to invest in a data integration strategy. Right timing depends on the data science of the organization, the application of limited resources to data, and the ability to take advantage of the data. If these factors don't add up, the data will just accumulate in Hadoop, costing money, and giving both the data and the people who did the integration a black eye in the process.

Grow the data science of the organization. That is the demand of the supply of data you will provide to your organization by integrating data in Hadoop.

2. Integrating Data into Hadoop for an Enterprise Data Repository

This is a specific application that relates to Mistake #1.

For the cost of storing data (which is a lousy way of analyzing a workload), Hadoop is relatively cheap, followed by a data warehouse/data appliance or specialized RDBMS, followed by the relational database management system. Functionality follows price.

A mistake that many are making is to look to lock-and-load a perfectly fine RDBMS data warehouses into Hadoop, while ignoring new uses of data (or just new data) that do make sense for Hadoop. And while all company data should be stored somewhere, it does not follow that all of it should reside in one platform.

The enterprise data warehouse is best thought of as integrated parts, with at least one of them being a bigger-than-the-rest relational enterprise data warehouse, and at least one of them being a Hadoop cluster. All components work together with the data integration and data virtualization described in this book.

The so-called all-encompassing "data lake" could comprise one of the Hadoop clusters, but it also needs to have a business purpose. There is a need for the data lake concept in many modern environments. Sharing the cluster and the tools across different data sets and subject areas brings many benefits.

Sharing the data, as long as concurrency is not a technical issue, is nothing but beneficial. Sharing a platform means departments with smaller budgets can still get their data from a robust platform and not have to go through their own acquisition and provisioning. It means you don't have each group building Hadoop clusters in their own way.

Any Hadoop cluster will, at most, coexist with its less expensive per-capita server farms, processing large amounts of unstructured data. The cluster will pass some of it to relational systems with broader capabilities, while those relational systems continue to do much of an enterprise's processing—especially of structured data.

3. Overemphasis on Data Integration Performance to the Detriment of Query Performance for Data Usage

Technical architects have to load data. The volume of data coming into a Hadoop cluster is often so incredibly high (compared to that of the data warehouse) that there tends to be a high focus on the early steps of the data value chain (data integration) to the detriment of the later steps (data access).

Fortunately, Hadoop can usually "drag along" great query performance with its great (if using the techniques described herein) load performance. But, not always.

There are myriad ways to access Hadoop data. They are all going to be restricted by the Hadoop architecture, which favors a batch-like approach to access, leading to performance gains increasing exponentially with data volume. Small jobs can seem to take inordinately long on Hadoop, regardless of the tool used.

Then there is Hive, which is very limited and slow. Hive queries are converted into MapReduce jobs by split creation, record generation, and mapper generation. If you create a great Hadoop "back end" and put Hive on it for the users, you may ruin the whole value proposition.

Furthermore, there are data visualization tools like Tableau and Qlikview, which abstract the "filesystem" backend. Then, through HCatalog and other means of understanding the data, the data may be viewed as Sparklines, Bullet Graphs, Scatter Plots, Treemaps, Background Mapping, InfoGraphics, and the like.

Good Data Visualization:

- Helps people find relationships in the data
- Does not distort data
- Meets expectations with information
- Is sufficiently detailed
- Leads to action
- Uses familiar icons, colors, and arrangements.

Finally, there is the emerging SQL-on-Hadoop category, where Hadoop and the SQL engine are on the same cluster, using the same nodes to store and process data. These tools are the best of all the "accessible" ways to access Hadoop data. They can also leverage existing skill sets. Even so, it matters which SQL-on-Hadoop tool is chosen. Considerations include:

- The SQL commands available, especially around joins
- User-defined function capabilities
- The translation capabilities of Hadoop data to relational data to work with SQL
- Concurrency management.

Give users the best way—with big data, this means the highest performance and best visualization—to access data in Hadoop clusters, and be sure to design the data for use. This leads us to the next mistake.

4. Not Refining Data to the Point of Usefulness

Integrating data into Hadoop clusters can bring about challenges similar to those we have in the relational world: we build it and they do not come. The fact that we are working with more sophisticated Hadoop users could lead us to build a cluster just for the advanced-user community.

However, data systems seldom will achieve full reach, activation, and returns by focusing on that crowd. Stepping down from the sophistication of the early Hadoop user, we find the analysts and business leaders who just want answers from data. Lying beneath the initial early adopter Hadoop users are hordes of future users, too many for the Hadoop build team to manage individually. Therefore, the Hadoop data must be usable without phone calls, uncertainty, or difficulty.

Don't forget the "T" in ELT (see Chapter 3) and feel free to refine data beyond its original form. This could include creating summarizations, derivations, aggregations, and data corrections.

5. Improper Node Specification

Data integration on a poorly-defined cluster will suffer. The cluster is formed from a number of nodes, node specifications, and potential striping across data centers.

Practically, Hadoop is thought of as "scale-out." This could mean that you focus your scaling energies on "how many?" as opposed to "what specification?" Increasingly, we are challenging the notion of *ignoring node specification to focus scaling exclusively on scale-out.*

Most clusters can contain nodes of varying specifications. Since nodes are built out over time in agile fashion, it logically follows that nodes have multiple specifications. While this introduces potential performance variation, better-specified nodes—even though they may not be practical to deploy throughout the cluster—will yield better selective performance and incorporate new lessons into your Hadoop journey. In other words, no environment should truly be thought of as entirely scale-out.

The goal is not to just check the "scale-out" box, but to benefit from its true advantages.

Many enterprise platforms that were formerly focused on scaling up now can scale out and make multiple nodes work together. This is admittedly a vastly different scale-out ratio than that of most Hadoop or NoSQL clusters. We're talking scaling out to eight nodes, for example, instead of hundreds. In these clusters, pay careful attention to the specification of each node.

A Hadoop cluster requires a balance between hard drive count, CPU core count, and memory density. When buying, consider different CPU technologies and CPU bus speeds, data and infrastructure node memory allocations, and types of hard drive controllers. The correct balance and budget depends on anticipated usage, performance expectations, and data activity/temperature. Be sure to get some outside, forward-looking perspectives on these 'anticipated' aspects of your Hadoop workload.

Too often, clusters are put together with the thought, "Hadoop is so much better for the workload, and the specification of the cluster itself is not important." Here is some guidance on specifying a data node in a cluster—once you get to that point by determining cluster size. Note that we are not referring to administrative nodes like name nodes, trackers, standby name nodes, or high availability nodes.

- **Architect with at least one spindle per core**, with each spindle as a separate file system. I/O bound workloads could use more spindles per core. The optimization of the nodes for I/O or CPU is an important one and requires a good visioning of the eventual workloads.

- **Use large drives**—a terabyte minimum. This assumes you have at least three terabytes to manage in the cluster. Since Hadoop workloads tend to be large sequential I/O scans, the lower seek times in larger drives is usually a good tradeoff.
- **Use dual multi-core CPUs** running 2.5 GHz.
- **Have at least 64MB of memory per node.** This will work even if you want to use HBase. This much memory combined with somewhere between 12-20 cores per node will allow for dozens of concurrent tasks.

6. Over-Reliance on Open Source Hadoop

While you could download the Hadoop source tarballs from Apache yourself, the main benefit of commercial Hadoop distributions is that they assemble the various open source projects from Apache, and test and certify the countless new releases together. They are presented as a package such as Hortonworks Data Platform 2.3. These packages save businesses the costs of testing and assembling for the science project, since it will take more than HDFS and MapReduce to establish Hadoop in an enterprise. Given version dependencies, the process of assembling the components can be time-consuming.

Vendors also provide additional enhancements to the open source software, such as support, consulting, and training. One area lacking for enterprises in the open source-only software is tools that help administrators configure, monitor, and manage Hadoop.

Another area of need is enterprise integration. Just as they do with other enterprise systems, commercial distributions provide additional connectors of availability, scalability, and reliability.

These are well covered by the major commercial distributions. Some of the vendors push their wares back into the open source en masse, while others do not. Proceed with caution to avoid a "Top 10 Mistake."

When selecting how you will deploy Hadoop for the enterprise, keep in mind the process for getting it into production. You can spend equal time developing and productionalizing if you do not use a commercial distribution. Since you are already saving tremendous dollars in data storage by going with Hadoop (over a relational database), some expenditure for a commercial distribution can be worthwhile.

7. ETL instead of ELT

Chapter 3 deals with the data integration architectural style decision. As a "mistake," it can cost you speed and flexibility to go with an ETL approach for loading a Hadoop cluster.

When using ETL, the transformations are processed by an ETL tool. On the contrary, with an ELT approach, the transformations are processed in the cluster. With ELT, the raw data can remain in the cluster for a long time and data can be subsequently transformed, unburdened by a legacy transformation decision that is prohibitive to that use.

Hadoop is a strong processing engine with scale-out good hardware and heavy processing can be performed there.

8. Using MapReduce to Load Hadoop

Leveraging Spark directly gives a clear advantage in the ability to process increasingly larger datasets.

When the size of the datasets are relatively small (i.e. less than three million transactional records and 5GB log files), the difference in execution time will be negligible, because MapReduce and Spark approaches are able to complete the jobs quickly. However, once the data grows, the difference will become impactful.

Increasing execution times will be frustrating for analysts and data scientists who are eager to conduct their data experiments and advanced analytics, but will be left to wait a day for their target datasets to be integrated. The addition of complexities in the mappings (multiple lookup keys) will further exacerbate the concern. By using MapReduce, a lookup transformation digs a large performance hole for itself as the lookup data cache and index cache get overwhelmed.

By leveraging the in-memory capabilities of Spark, users can integrate datasets at much faster rates. Spark uses fast Remote Procedure Calls for efficient task dispatching and scheduling. It also leverages a thread pool for execution of tasks rather than a pool of Java Virtual Machine processes. This enables Spark to schedule and execute tasks at rates measured in milliseconds, whereas MapReduce scheduling takes seconds and sometimes minutes in busy clusters.

9. Using Spark through Hive to Load Hadoop

Spark through Hive would not be an ideal approach resulting in the best Spark results. Execution results would be inconsistent to indefinite. Developing a good use of Spark for a vendor is not dissimilar to developing the product initially. It takes years and millions of dollars.

Utilizing the full capability of Spark for Data Integration with Hadoop, as Talend Big Data does, is a winning approach.

10. Ignoring the Quality of the Data Being Loaded

As Chapter 5 pointed out, poor data quality can easily be disguised by the massive volumes of data, leading to "quantity over quality" thinking. Big data is still data, and data will still be processed by systems and humans. Those actions will be only as good as the input—the data.

We recommend spot reviewing the data against any business expectations, from perspectives of completeness, accuracy, and conformance. Where violations are found, systemically correct them in the ELT, or better yet, at the source.

Those who load Hadoop are not loading "widget" data. They must be as familiar with the contents they are injecting into the organization as they are with the Hadoop setup itself.

11 Case Studies and Trends

Case Studies in Big Data Integration

Payment Processing

I spoke with Aaron Werman, the Director of Big Data and Database Innovation at a major payment processing company, about the introduction and use of Hadoop in their data management environment. The company provides a seamless experience to merchants, allowing various payment forms. There's a high chance that your last credit card authorization was processed by their gateways.

How they use Hadoop

The company has built a data lake in Hadoop (Cloudera distribution). They are not standardizing the data; there is no ETL. The "ingest reflects exactly the data as visible in source," according to Werman. It involves transactional data collection with light formatting. A self-described "ETL hater," Werman wanted to be sure to make *all* the data available: "ETL is reeling now because their stuff can be done in Hadoop environments."

Whenever we ask about Hadoop use, we always do so in context of the (relational) data warehouse(s), since Hadoop generally serves a similar function. However, at Aaron's company, there is not a structure they would consider a data warehouse. They have an "EDW lite," but it does not have the conforming dimensions, enterprise models, master data, or other attributes of a true data warehouse.

They use the data lake for two forms of analytics:

1. **Inward Analytics**–Pushing necessary processing to a less expensive platform to reduce the cost. This is a good approach not only for the reduced cost of processing, but also for the reduced cost of programming, since some operational systems are difficult to change. Werman observed, "Hadoop has dropped the cost envelope; for example, over 90% on data storage. This allows us to keep all of our data cost effectively."
2. **Analytical products** as part of the company portfolio– These products are data products and are based on the data collected in their data lake.

How they Load Data into Hadoop

Initially, they were using a combination of Kafka (a message broker) and Spark. However, they are now executing all new loads with Talend Big Data and Talend Studio 6.1. They use Talend with all source types, including relational databases, flat files, and message buses. These comprise hundreds of feeds over dozens of systems. The load is currently about 1 terabyte per day—500 billion records. They have established "patterns" for each type, making it easy to replicate for future sources of the same type.

By bringing a robust data integration tool together with a Hadoop distribution from an established provider, they mitigate the risk of having an enormous skill gap. Data integration developers have long used data integration tools, and can readily adopt their skills to the Hadoop environment with Talend.

Tips, Tricks, and Trends

They have not yet migrated to Talend Spark, but it is on their roadmap. While "difficult" to do, there is a lot of code being committed to Spark, and it will be worth it. They look forward to Spark 2.0, which is on the Talend roadmap.

Werman cited the enormous value of the data lake and the use of a tool like Talend in the process of building the data lake.

"Invest in Impala [Cloudera's open source massively parallel processing (MPP) SQL query engine] for fast query. ETL tools play nicely with it and combining it with Parquet [a columnar storage format for Hadoop] is a great option compared to Hive. One caution on this approach is that Parquet is not supported by Sqoop and data has to get dumped into an intermediate form."

Werman saw the big data integration landscape as having two lanes within the Architecture: a real-time fast lane and a batch processing slow lane. While the real-time and streaming use cases in the fast lane are receiving all the attention, he sees a middle lane he calls the "immediate access" lane, which he describes as being dominated by Impala and faster querying abilities. He sees the most value for his organization in making data quickly available to the business by whatever means necessary, which is a different take than being focused on how data is sourced and loaded (i.e. batch or streaming).

Finally, as they have done, Werner recommends building patterns in Talend for common data source types.

Healthcare

I spoke with the Vice President of Information Management at a leading on-demand healthcare concierge service.

How They use Hadoop

The VP joined the company in 2014 and was chartered with reinvigorating the company technology, with a focus on the legacy infrastructure. He knew Hadoop had to be part of the equation.

They use Hadoop (Hortonworks distribution on AWS) for data archiving and data science. Though in production, flexibility is built into the processes to allow Hadoop to achieve the flexibility (think sandbox) that a data science lab requires. Their plan for Hadoop is to load data in real time, which differs from the process of their (and most) data warehouses, which by necessity will remain batch loaded.

The sources of data are claims (200,000 per day), membership, and eligibility data. Due to the nature of the business, this is not data internally generated. As the files are made accessible, this external data is connected directly with Talend. As they continue to grow their source environment, and reach back into more history, the data will grow. Currently it's a terabyte. You don't need "big data" for Hadoop to make sense.

Data is processed in Hadoop and passed to the data warehouse in a "data refinery" style of Hadoop usage pattern. They also load their master data (from MDM) into the Hadoop cluster to facilitate its access there.

Teams and Technologies

The development team comprises 12 people total, supporting the entire data infrastructure. In particular, they support the data scientists of the organization, who are recent hires. The data scientists are currently using R, primarily.

The team uses Talend Big Data to load Hadoop. They also have Talend MDM and Data Quality in the company. They like reusing data integration tool skills in the Hadoop environment. Talend allows for the leveraging of existing skills (and avoiding MapReduce) in the database environment.

Incidentally, they did not start with Talend open source, but started with the enterprise edition. Though not measured, Talend gives them "fast" performance; they intend to utilize the Talend relational tools in the legacy environment. As with Aaron, they have not yet migrated to Spark, but it is on their roadmap.

Tips, Tricks, and Trends

He suggests thinking about how data will be used before beginning indiscriminate collection. This is consistent with the advice of this book, and it clearly puts them into a more confident position beginning the Hadoop journey.

He also advised: "Understand the landscape of Hadoop and leverage the best." The Hadoop ecosystem is still undergoing change and expansion; a company shouldn't enter it until they're equipped with a good understanding.

Finally, although it works well and is worth it, he notes that establishing a Hadoop cluster in AWS is a lot of work. Be prepared for it. They spent copious time in the security layer.

Trends in Hadoop and Summary of Ideas

The idea of scale-out file systems that may be lacking in functionality, but can handle modern levels of complex data, is here to stay. Hadoop is the epitome of that idea. Although it has been pivoted a few times, its simple file system (HDFS) remains, and quite the ecosystem is building up around it.

While there used to be little overlap between reasonable selection of Hadoop and reasonable selection of a DBMS, that has changed. Hadoop has withstood the test of time and has grown to the point where quite a few applications platformed on a DBMS will be "offloaded" to Hadoop. The cost savings, combined with the ability to execute the complete application, will be persuasive. Inside of some organizations, a figurative levee will break, and Hadoop will quickly gain market share. Hadoop is not just for big data anymore.

Although Hadoop is not usually referred to as a "NoSQL" data store, it shares with NoSQL systems a similarity in that it was not built for SQL. However, it's clear that SQL is robust and knowledge of it is entrenched in the community. As such, both Hadoop and the NoSQL camps have seen an emergence of tools that use SQL, or something close to SQL. We must also include data virtualization tools that span systems in a query as a member of the SQL camp. SQL is clearly here to stay.

With unprecedented global contribution and interest, Spark is moving quickly to become the method of choice for data access in HDFS (as well as other storage formats). Users have demanded improved performance and Spark offers exactly that. While the node specification is in the hands of the users, Spark provides the perfect balance between cost and performance. This clearly makes Hadoop much more than cold storage, and opens it up to a multitude of processing possibilities.

As discussed in Chapter 8, streaming data will be increasingly leveraged for real-time use cases like fraud detection, next best offer, telemetrics, authorizations, and Internet of Things applications. A data integration tool that can handle streaming data is a must today.

Hadoop usage has evolved since the early days when the technology was invented to make the batch processing of big data affordable and scalable. Today, with a lively community of open source contributors and vendors innovating a plethora of tools that natively support Hadoop components, usage and data is expanding.

Loading Hadoop Clusters will Continue to be a Top Job at Companies Far and Wide

Traditionally data preparation has consumed an estimated 80% of analytic development efforts. As in the relational database world, many organizations prefer ELT processes, where higher performance is achieved by performing transformations after loading. Instead of burdening the data warehouse with this processing, data is transformed in Hadoop. This yields high-performance, fault-tolerant, elastic processing without detracting from query speeds.

Since being limited by low-performing open source Sqoop, Flume, command line HDFS, and Hive in the early days, numerous approaches and tools have been developed to meet the Hadoop data integration challenge.

Many enterprises are bringing the features and functions they are accustomed to in the relational world into the Hadoop world, as well as the non-functional requirements, developer productivity, metadata management, documentation, and business rules management that a modern data integration tool provides. Tools that leverage Spark directly, use ELT, and support streaming data give a clear advantage in the ability to process the increasingly larger datasets in business today.

Index

www.ingramcontent.com/pod-product-compliance
Lightning Source LLC
Chambersburg PA
CBHW070836070326
40690CB00009B/1574